EXPERT
LEADERSHIP

HOW ENTREPRENEURS ARE LEADING THE FUTURE IN MIND, MASTERY, AND MEANING

EXPERT
LEADERSHIP

How Entrepreneurs Are Leading the Future in Mind, Mastery, and Meaning

— Written by —

Rob Kosberg • R.J. De Rossi • Jennifer Knowles • Nick Grubiša • Angela Sutton, PhD
Greg Mohr • Sharise M. Bijou, MSA, MSW, LCSW • Neil Gordon • Rachael Draper, PhD
Mark Carpenter • David R. Clark • Jan Schaffner • Dennis Duff, MSU & Ellen Eatough, MA
Andrew A. Wittig • J.R. Vincent • Robert Aymar • Dr. Benjamin Koen

BEST SELLER PUBLISHING

Published by Best Seller Publishing®, St. Augustine, FL
Best Seller Publishing® is a registered trademark.
Printed in the United States of America.
ISBN: 9781966395485

For more information, please write:
Best Seller Publishing®
53 Marine Street
St. Augustine, FL 32084
or call 1 (626) 765-9750

Visit us online at:
www.BestSellerPublishing.org

For more information regarding our authors,
please visit BestSellerPublishing.org/ExpertLeadership

TABLE OF CONTENTS

ABOUT ROB KOSBERG

Rob Kosberg is a Wall Street Journal and USA Today best-selling author, founder of Best Seller Publishing, and has been featured on ABC, NBC, CBS, FOX, as well as hundreds of other publications, podcasts, and media outlets. Rob has spoken to and taught tens of thousands of entrepreneurs, coaches, and consultants how to stop hunting for clients and instead position themselves as the hunted.

For more information regarding our authors, please visit our webpage!
BestSellerPublishing.org/ExpertLeadership

WHY LEADERSHIP MATTERS NOW MORE THAN EVER

BY ROB KOSBERG

Leadership. It's one of those words that gets tossed around so much that it risks becoming a buzzword. Yet, when you strip away the jargon and job titles, leadership is what defines whether companies thrive or collapse, whether communities unite or fragment, whether the future is one we create intentionally or one we stumble into.

Walk into any boardroom, startup, nonprofit, or even a family dinner, and you'll see it plain as day: leadership, or the lack thereof, is shaping the outcomes. It's the silent force behind every movement, merger, mission, or moment of breakthrough. Whether you're steering a Fortune 500 company or mentoring the next generation at your local rec center, your leadership — or how you show up for others — sets the tone.

At different times in my own business life, I've found myself under harsh leadership. Maybe you have too. It's one thing to endure it; it's another not to imitate it. It's far too easy to absorb those patterns and replicate them without realizing it. Learning to lead differently, to lead with empathy, clarity, and purpose — has been one of my greatest challenges and greatest rewards.

That's why this book matters. That's why leadership matters.

We're living through an era that feels more complex, fast-paced, and uncertain than ever before. Technological disruption, societal shifts, economic turbulence — every leader today faces an evolving landscape where yesterday's playbook no longer applies. What worked in the industrial age faltered in the information age and is now obsolete in the age of AI, remote work, and social consciousness.

And so, this anthology, *Expert Leadership: How Entrepreneurs Are Leading the Future in Mind, Mastery, and Meaning*, is both a reflection of where leadership stands today — and a challenge to where it could go next.

WHY WE WROTE THIS BOOK

The purpose of this collection is simple: to gather the voices of those who are not just theorizing about leadership but living it out in the trenches. Entrepreneurs, executives, innovators, consultants, and thought leaders — each of the contributors in this book has weathered storms, overcome challenges, and reshaped teams, companies, and communities.

But more importantly, they've done it in a world where leadership is no longer about barking orders from the top of the hierarchy. The modern leader needs to be more than a manager of tasks or a motivator of people. Today's leader is a creator of cultures, a builder of systems, and a steward of purpose.

This book will give you insights into how leadership is evolving. It's about agility, resilience, and humanity. It's about leading teams who crave not just direction but connection. It's about navigating the complexities of our time with clarity and courage.

We've anchored this anthology in three core themes: Mind, Mastery, and Meaning — the pillars that every leader must cultivate.

- **Mind** speaks to mindset, emotional intelligence, and self-awareness. Because you can't lead others until you know how to lead yourself.

- **Mastery** is about skill. It's about the hard-won lessons, the frameworks, the strategies, and the tactical approaches that help leaders drive results in real time.

- **Meaning** is about purpose. It's the why behind the what. Today's best leaders inspire loyalty and spark innovation because they tap into something deeper — mission, values, legacy.

Why This Anthology Is Different

This isn't another leadership book written in a vacuum. The power here lies in the range of contributors and the variety of perspectives you'll encounter.

In these pages, you'll hear from entrepreneurs who've built businesses from scratch — and from executives leading teams inside billion-dollar organizations. You'll learn from franchise pioneers, C-suite coaches, and thought leaders who've walked the tightrope of leadership in both the corporate world and the chaotic, uncertain world of startups.

Each voice brings you something real — stories from the trenches, frameworks forged in fire, strategies that have been tested under pressure.

You're not just getting inspiration here. You're getting insight and action. These contributors didn't just read about leadership — they lived it, failed at it, course-corrected, and emerged stronger. They're here to pass on those lessons to you.

If you want platitudes, go scroll your LinkedIn feed. If you want practical wisdom rooted in experience — this book is for you.

Leadership as a Journey, Not a Destination

Here's the truth: leadership is not a title, and it's never a finished product.

It's a lifelong journey of learning, reflection, and evolution. There's no "I've arrived" moment. The most effective leaders I know are the ones who stay humble, stay curious, and stay adaptable. They're willing to be wrong. They're willing to reimagine their approach when the game changes — and in today's world, the game is changing daily.

That's why this book isn't just about theory or frameworks. It's also about mindset. We're inviting you, the reader, to reflect deeply on your own leadership path. Where are you growing? Where are you stuck? Where are you thriving — and where might you be holding back?

You'll find chapters here that will challenge you, encourage you, and maybe even call you out. That's a good thing. Because great leadership starts with the courage to look inward before you step up to lead outward.

Your Call to Action

So, here's what I'd encourage you to do as you dive into this anthology:

- Don't just read — engage. Grab a pen, scribble notes, underline what resonates.

- Apply what you learn. Whether it's a leadership tactic, a communication framework, or a mindset shift, try it out with your team, your clients, or even your family.

- Reflect often. Leadership is situational, and what you take from this book today might land differently when you revisit it a year from now.

The world doesn't just need more leaders. The world needs better leaders. Leaders who are present, principled, and prepared to meet this moment — and the next — with heart and clarity.

Welcome to Expert Leadership.

Let's get to work.

EXPERT
LEADERSHIP

How Entrepreneurs Are Leading the Future in Mind, Mastery, and Meaning

— Written by —

Rob Kosberg • R.J. De Rossi • Jennifer Knowles • Nick Grubiša • Angela Sutton, PhD
Greg Mohr • Sharise M. Bijou, MSA, MSW, LCSW • Neil Gordon • Rachael Draper, PhD
Mark Carpenter • David R. Clark • Jan Schaffner • Dennis Duff, MSU & Ellen Eatough, MA
Andrew A. Wittig • J.R. Vincent • Robert Aymar • Dr. Benjamin Koen

About R.J. De Rossi

R.J. De Rossi is a leadership educator, executive coach, speaker, and international best-selling author of *Broken Places: A Sacred Journey of Repair*.

He blends neuroscience-informed practices, peacebuilding, emotional intelligence, and flow psychology to support personal resilience and collective healing. His work bridges mindfulness, peak performance, and purpose-driven leadership.

A certified nonviolence trainer with two decades of experience teaching and leading teams in education and brain injury rehabilitation, R.J. brings a soulful lens to leadership, helping people find clarity, connection, and creative purpose.

Rooted in storytelling and wisdom traditions — and a self-proclaimed seminary school dropout — he offers seminars, workshops, keynotes, and media appearances on leadership, meditation, conflict reconciliation, collaborative culture, and applied spirituality.

He hosts *The R.J. De Rossi Show: Life Meaning Repair* podcast and writes *The Work of Love: Letters from the Heart of Servant Leadership*, a LinkedIn column exploring leadership as a soulful, transformative practice.

When he's not writing or speaking, he's binge-watching sci-fi, doodling, or cuddling with his cat babies, Rocco and Oliver.

For more information regarding our authors,
please visit our webpage!
BestSellerPublishing.org/ExpertLeadership

CHAPTER 1

LEADERSHIP IS HARD AS HELL, BUT IT GETS EASIER

(A SURVIVAL GUIDE)

BY R.J. DE ROSSI

Do it until you can't do it anymore. That's what Sophie said.

"Don't quit just because it's hard," she told me. "Six months ago, I was exactly where you are now."

Bullshit, I thought. *No one could be as bad at this as I am.*

She added, "Leadership is hard as hell," then paused for dramatic flair. "But it gets easier."

Sophie was the director of Ventura NeuroHope, a traumatic brain injury (TBI) rehab facility and sister location to the facility I directed. Our regional director, Bill — a former beat cop turned night nurse turned corporate puppet master — had hooked Sophie and me up as "work buddies," part of my on-the-job training as the new director of the Anaheim site. His advice was scant: "Do your job. And be kind."

Sophie, a New York transplant, spewed a frenetic energy that both enticed and exhausted you. Quick-witted, fashionable, and drop-dead gorgeous, she possessed a brazen edge I envied. There were no apologies about her. At the time we were introduced, she had Airbnb'd her apartment and was living full-time at a local casino, a high roller enjoying free hotel rooms and surf-and-turf dinners. Most of her work was done remotely through her cellphone. During our daily calls, I'd hear a digital cacophony of slot machines as she juggled gambling, texting her staff, and dispensing hard-boiled wisdom. It was as if she'd stepped straight out of a Mafia movie — Al Capone in stilettos and rouge.

Sophie was also my secret agent. I picked her brain for everything from company policies to management tactics, even the scoop on the best New York pizza in California — which she assured me was a lost cause! Her invisible hand gave me a way to save face in front of my staff, who were gobsmacked over Bill's decision to hire me, a TBI newbie. My predecessor had been a 35-year veteran director. And yet, despite that expertise, NeuroHope was barely hanging on, with a critically low census. "Get 'heads in beds' and avoid permanent closure," Bill warned. No pressure.

Honestly, the whole situation baffled me. *Why me?* As a teacher, I had led a school-wide conflict mediation program at a K–12 school for "behavior" kids. So leadership and communication, I knew. Brain injury? Not so much. Even during my interview, I spent more time arguing *against* my candidacy than for it. To no avail.

"Learning technical knowledge is easy," Bill said. "Finding raw talent isn't. Besides, we're opening behavior modification schools in the near future. Once you learn the ropes, you can oversee that project as regional director."

Thus, I was offered the gig, complete with 24/7 on-call responsibility. Apparently, it was a short list because no one in their right mind wants that kind of commitment. But since those schools were on the table — and I'm not always in my right mind! — I went for it.

How bad could it be?

REALITY SLAP

Pretty bad, actually.

Day one was a reality slap. Inside, wood-paneled walls and a heavy blanket of tension in the air dampened my "first-day-of-school" butter-flies as soon as I walked in. It was as if I'd stepped into a time warp, a 1970s photo. The only things missing were avocado-green appliances and a retractable spinning disco ball.

Although the team was friendly enough to me, they seemed … edgy. Inauthentic. I couldn't quite put my finger on why. Twenty minutes in, a staff member approached me, informing me that one of the patients, who'd recently undergone cranioplasty surgery to replace his missing skull section, had clear liquid running from his nose. Worried it could be a cranial fluid leak, she asked me if she should call the paramedics. I froze in place, as if she'd tagged me in a game of freeze tag.

"Floundering" doesn't begin to describe my performance. I puzzled my way through insolvable jargon like aphasia, hemiparesis, and benign paroxysmal positional vertigo. Forgetting tasks, tripping over my tongue, and more freezing during emergency situations became regular, on-brand occurrences for me. During meetings, the clinical team would dominate and dismiss me as if I were some bubble-headed intern. (Which, in all fairness, from their perspective, I was.)

Although I was pulling out all the stops — a 90-minute-long commute, constant night and weekend calls, pulling all-nighters because of graveyard shift staff call-outs — the arrows of castigation continuously flew in from my staff. Unqualified. Unprepared. Unprofessional. And on and on …

I had literally written a book on forgiveness and reconciliation. I'd trained corporations on empathic leadership and team flow. Yet, here I was — jumpy, defensive, and on the counterattack — like some hybrid snapping turtle-shrew straight from the *Island of Dr. Moreau*.

The worst part, though, was the utter lack of joy — the black hole sucking all the creative juices out of me. As a teacher, I'd infused my classroom with corny dad jokes and free-flowing spontaneity, and the kids had thrived on it. I had thrived on it. But here, these old goats were grim, humorless, and unimpressed by my schtick. Total crickets. I found myself twisting into pretzel shapes all day, like some insecure yogi, desperately trying to fit into a cardboard cutout of their expectations.

One afternoon, Michelle, our longtime physical therapist, popped off at me in the kitchen. I knew why. Our caseload had spiked, leaving us understaffed and overwhelmed. And then there were my remote Fridays I'd negotiated when I was hired — my chance to escape a day of traffic hell and focus on admin tasks. My team was pissed about both.

Michelle was the de facto ringleader at my facility, often barking fast orders to staff and openly defying me. Built like a volleyball middle blocker, the fact was, she scared the hell outta me. Our public spats had become an embarrassing pattern by this point, the seeds of confusion sown, no one quite sure who the real boss was. They just couldn't — wouldn't — trust me as a leader or let me in their circle. I was an outsider. A step-parent.

"Your Michelle sounds like my Linda," Sophie said. "She's always pushing back. You know what my response is every time? 'Linda, just be cool. Can you do that for me?'"

"Does that work?" I asked.

"It shuts her up until her next episode," Sophie said.

Just be cool. Hmm. Sounded like sage advice. But maybe it was me, not Michelle, who needed to chill. Blaming everyone and everything — including myself! — for my ineptitude was turning out to be a toxic feedback loop. I needed to find my own version of "just be cool." One that let me and everyone else off the hook. One that secured my emotional footing and, hopefully, lured my team into some semblance of functionality.

Later that week, during my usual call with Sophie, I had news for her: "Bill just emailed. The schools aren't even happening anymore. I need to level with my team, admit that I'm failing them. Figure out my next move. It's like the Universe is conspiring against me ..."

"You're not failing," she said. "Just let them know who's in charge. And it's not Michelle. Keep pushing. Eventually they'll quit, and you can hire new staff who'll actually respect you. The secret to success is simple: be the last man standing."

Too late, I thought. *I'm already flat on my ass.*

"No," I said firmly. "I need to do this my way. I'm tired of fighting."

WHAT REALLY MATTERS

Then Michelle's mother died.

I remembered when my own mother passed, and a controlling supervisor I often clashed with attended the wake, even cooked a meal for my family and me during our darkest hours. I never saw him the same way again. I wanted to offer Michelle the same comfort. I attended her mother's celebration of life ceremony, sitting inconspicuously in the back row. As the family walked in, Michelle saw me and reached out. I held her forearm and leaned in for a warm hug. Here, she wasn't so imposing. Here, we were on common ground.

One by one, Michelle's family members stood up and shared hilarious and touching stories of their mother, nanny, sister, and auntie. This woman was a Titan — a bawdy, beer-swilling, sports-crazed, world-traveling lover of life *as it is*. No piety. No masks. No BS. Her home — a refuge for so many stray-cat vagabonds just passing through — was apparently where everyone ended up for the after-after party. And hell would surely freeze over if she ever missed a grandkid's football or volleyball game! *This* is where Michelle got her gusto.

I had gone to the services for Michelle, even with the sneaky hope of winning her over, but instead I left with a reminder of what really matters.

CLEARING THE AIR

It was time.

At the next all-staff meeting, I got real with my team. Spilled my guts and shared Bill's original plan for me, how I knew I was failing them, my vision for NeuroHope, my genuine desire for a better working relationship with them, and my decision to start looking for new work.

"I know I'm not the best leader," I said. "I hope I'm not the worst. But I believe I have a purpose here. I'm a natural visionary and connector — even if you haven't seen that side of me. You have a rich history. Maybe I can support your next chapter before I leave."

They looked both shocked and illumined. The dots were connecting, and it made some sense now — why Bill chose me, a former teacher, to step in.

"Only if you want," I added. "If not, I'll slide out quietly."

"What's your timeline?" Michelle asked.

Wow, I thought. *She can't wait for me to quit. Is she vying for my position?*

"I want to make a dent here first," I said. "Introduce new tech, ramp up professional development, and get funding for renovations."

More silence. Then Michelle asked, "How can I help?"

A GOOD PLACE

Over the next few months, Michelle and I met weekly to implement our vision. She was still full of fire, but more respectful, deferential even. Thank God. And, yes, we even filled those beds, breaking our census records. I could hire additional staff to round out our team. I secured pay raises for our lower-waged employees. I treated everyone to monthly luncheons. (As we used to say in education, "If you don't feed the teachers, they'll eat the students!") I even struck a deal with Bill for renovation funds to overhaul the on-site gym!

It wasn't perfect. Nothing ever is. I was still "too soft," as Sophie would say, and still wasn't enthralled with the TBI world — but I focused on relationships. We all still had our personality clashes under stress, but as Michelle admitted to me, "We're in a good place." The words were medicine to my soul. Somehow, we'd shifted from a dysfunctional battleground to a neurotic work family.

But as my professional universe was expanding, Sophie's was collapsing.

BROKEN RECORD GURU

"This is it," Sophie said, her tone even edgier than usual.

"What do you mean?" I asked.

"Bill's been promoted," she said. "His replacement isn't going to get me. I give it a month."

Sophie could jump from zero to "the sky is falling" on a frenzied whim.

From that day on, our relationship shifted. Gradually, she began turning to *me* for counsel during our recaps, seeking advice on communication and emotional regulation.

As Sophie's mentor, I was a broken record guru with a singular mantra: "Don't do anything when you're pissed. Wait until you're calm. Then you'll think clearly and act accordingly."

When she'd rant about her staff or our new supervisor, I started up a little game called "Five Innocent Reasons" to help soften her views. The rules were simple: come up with five plausible reasons why someone's acting like a jerk. Right or wrong, it didn't matter — it was just an exercise in reinterpretation.

"Can't we just play 'Five Scandalous Reasons' instead?!" she'd joke.

I'd respond, almost fatherly, "Nope, rules are rules."

WHAT WOULD SOPHIE SAY?

A few months later, Sophie was, indeed, fired. She had gone off on our new regional director during a facility visit.

Fury bubbled up inside me. Why couldn't she have just kept her mouth shut?! Why is everything all or nothing?! Now what am I supposed to do?

With my shadow advisor sacked, I started asking myself, "What would Sophie say?" hoping to tap into my own inner Sophie — a courageous know-it-all badass. Although she was still a resource behind the scenes, I felt horrible asking for help while her world was crumbling. But really, by then, I had secured my sea legs and finally had a handle on things. I just needed to trust myself.

When Sophie finally landed a new job, she was let go after only a few months. Same issue: her shoot-from-the-hip leadership style.

"Sophie, you gotta get a grasp on that. Relationships are the foundation for everything," I pleaded. "Especially in leadership."

"Are they, though?" was her skeptical response. "I'm a fighter. I'll get out of this. I always do." But then her overconfidence wobbled: "What's wrong with me? Am I cursed?"

"Nothing's wrong with you," I said. "You just can't act on every red-hot thought that fires in your head. Everything isn't a fight."

I'd learned a trick about outwitting Sophie's ego because she often bristled at pithy slogans and common clichés. I just had to use her words against her — that way she could finally hear me.

"I have a question," I told her. "What would Sophie say?"

"I don't know," she said, frustration rising in her tone. "Drive into a cement wall and end it all?"

"Just be cool. Can you do that for me?" I said, hoping the joke would land.

And Sophie laughed, a wild laugh with brambles in it.

"Touché," she countered. "Not my strong suit, but you're right. Well, *I'm* right! *Ha!* You've gotten good at this."

"I had a good mentor."

Sophie's brassy wit remained intact, even if she seemed a little weary now. Yet wiser and more self-possessed. I knew she'd be okay — just like I would be.

Sophie was right: leadership is hard as hell. A real fight for your life. A battle mostly fought within as we wrestle down our baser instincts. But, eventually, it does get easier. Sometimes, all we gotta do is ask, "What would Sophie say?" and not quit just because it's hard.

And, of course, just be cool.

For more information regarding our authors,
please visit our webpage!
BestSellerPublishing.org/ExpertLeadership

About Jennifer Knowles

Dr. Jennifer Knowles is a dynamic speaker, author, consultant, and professor dedicated to helping individuals and organizations unlock human potential and create impactful change. With a background in Organizational Development, a PhD in Organizational Learning, and a passion for authenticity and leadership, she blends academic insight with real-world experience — whether transforming corporate teams, advocating for youth entrepreneurship, or empowering women to lead with purpose.

For more information regarding our authors,
please visit our webpage!
BestSellerPublishing.org/ExpertLeadership

CHAPTER 2

FROM LEMONADE TO LEADERSHIP

(SIX LESSONS FOR SUCCESS)

BY JENNIFER KNOWLES

Two police officers approached my three young sons and me as we were selling lemonade in the park in front of our house.

"Lemonade?" my four-year-old stopped sipping away the profits long enough to ask the tall officer with a mustache.

"No, we're here to shut you down," the shorter officer said.

"Huh, why?" asked my six-year-old.

The officer spoke directly to me. "Do you have any permits? You need three permits to run a lemonade stand in Denver. And somebody complained about you."

"Permits for a children's lemonade stand? No, why would we have permits? And why would somebody complain about us?" I asked.

"They're required. You need to pack up your stuff and head home now. And somebody called you in," he said.

"This is one of their first lemonade stands, and they're raising money so they can sponsor a child in another country who needs help. Are you really being serious right now?"

"Sorry, lady. You've all got to go home now."

And that was that. We packed up our lemonade, table, and supplies, loaded them in the wagon, and headed home, heads hanging low.

As soon as we got inside in the house, we all crumpled on the stairs.

"What just happened, Mom? Why did they shut us down?" my oldest asked as he was fighting back tears. The other two boys started crying too.

"I don't know; apparently, we needed permits," I told them.

"Mama? What's a permit?" my youngest asked.

As I explained everything to the kids, I tried to stay strong. I couldn't believe what had just happened. They were raising money for charity. We were in front of our house. And who would have the nerve to call the cops on my kids?

I sighed, got on my phone, and searched online for permits for lemonade stands. Kids were subject to the same rules as adults. And permits were required for lemonade stands. Apparently, it *was* a thing. There were instances all across the country of kids' lemonade stands getting shut down by police. Long gone were the days from my childhood when kids could make lemonade and sell it to the community.

I thought about posting what happened to us on social media, complaining about our situation. But then I caught myself, thinking, "What good would that do?" So instead I went to bed.

At 2 a.m., I woke up out of a sound sleep with urgency and clarity. If I didn't know about these laws, surely others in our community didn't know either. I found the "Contact Us If You Have a Story" button on our local TV station websites and shared our story along with my contact information. Then I went back to bed.

At 6 a.m. the next morning, my phone rang.

"This is ABC 7. We saw your message. Can we be at your house at 8 a.m.?" the reporter asked. "And could you have your kids ready to talk too?"

"Uh, okay, sure, yes," I said, still half asleep. It took a moment for me to process what had just happened, and then I shot out of bed, realizing I had to get the kids up, fed, dressed, and camera-ready.

At 8 a.m. sharp, the reporter and a cameraman showed up at our doorstep. They spent about an hour with us, talking to the kids and me while getting lots of footage. They told us our news story would air on the local 12:00 p.m. news, and they were on their way.

Fast-forward 24 hours, and our story had gone viral. From coast to coast, our story was being shared. And I got my first invitation for my family to speak live on a major national news station for the morning show later that week.

We arrived at our local media station at 4 a.m. for our first national broadcast. The plan was that they would live stream us to the national station in NYC for a live interview to be streamed across the country. That is no small job when you've got three kids under eight years old who have to be there too. The producers greeted us, put powder on our faces, and sat us on stools in front of the camera view. They hooked us up to earphones and earpieces so we could hear the journalist talking to us from NYC. We looked straight at the camera even though there was nobody there.

Lights, camera, action!

The rest was a whirlwind. But after sharing what had happened, our focus pivoted to the following:

While the current laws banned kids' lemonade stands without permits, our plan was to change the laws.

Leadership Lemonade Lesson #1:

Rise above being a victim

Life throws us curveballs. We have a choice: Do we want live our life being a victim or a victor? When something happens that we don't foresee, do we turn failure into a hardship or turn failure into an opportunity?

Leadership Lemonade Lesson #2:

Don't be afraid to do big things

We can all do big things — we just have to find the courage to do so. I was terrified. What was I doing, going on live national TV with my kids? Why was I putting my family out there for the public to scrutinize?

But I had a strong *why*, that took big action to create change. What had happened to us was wrong, And if I didn't take a stand, who would? I had recently earned a PhD in Organizational Learning, Performance, and Change, and I had years of corporate experience. But I wasn't in politics; I wasn't in law. At that moment, I was a mama bear standing up for her kids in a very public way, and for kids throughout the community.

The next few weeks were a blur. We spoke on local radio stations, a local restaurant invited us to have a lemonade stand at their store, and the local charity we were initially raising money for invited us to have a lemonade stand at their headquarters. New stations were following us, and my family received attention we would have never dreamed of.

But you know what was the best part? Community. People from all walks of life reached out to us and wanted to support my kids, and all kids, and lemonade stands.

I caught wind that Kraft Heinz/Country Time Lemonade wanted to get in on the action. Why wouldn't one of the biggest lemonade selling companies want to help our cause?

I reached out via LinkedIn to the VP of Country Time Lemonade. We connected and agreed to help one another. We had a mutual cause — legalize lemonade stands. The company could get national attention and free marketing, and I could help support not only my kids' interest in lemonade stands, but help kids across the country.

But this came at a personal cost. Trolls sent me private messages. People who I thought were my friends iced me out. People were talking about my family, and it wasn't all favorable.

It was like I was standing on a tightrope, doing a balancing act, while people were trying to knock me off every step of the way.

Still, I continued. I reached out to my local city councilman in hope of changing the laws in my city. I left message after message with no response. Finally, I got through to him. His response was, "Just sit tight, we'll get to it."

Um ... no thanks. Don't tell me to sit tight. I'll find another way.

So I found another city councilman, a grandfatherly type, who seemed interested in the cause. I met him at a local coffee shop and shared with him that I was hoping to work with him to get the lemonade stand laws changed, and he said YES!

Leadership Lemonade Lesson #3:

When you face resistance, find another way

Leading through resistance is a common challenge among leaders. Some leaders thrive on conflict, but others become distressed by it. We need to learn to expect resistance, plan for it, and find ways through it.

Leadership Lemonade Lesson #4:

Build a community of people with a shared vision

A shared vision is a must when gathering support to create positive change. This provides everyone a clear idea of where they should be going. A clear purpose and vision can help weather any storm.

Together, the city councilman and I worked to propose a bill and gathered support in the community.

My boys and I provided public comments at city council meetings when they discussed the proposed city law change. And I brought the camera crew of the nationally syndicated news show *CBS This Morning* with me. That national attention certainly helped!

A few days later, the *Wall Street Journal* shared an article[1] about our mission: legalize lemonade stands. They focused on my kids and the work that Country Time Lemonade and I were advocating together, as well as highlighted examples of kids across the country who were facing similar challenges of having their lemonade stands shut down.

Soon after, Denver city council voted and passed the bill to legalize lemonade stands!

But our work was just getting started.

Next, I wanted to get the laws changed in the state. I looked up my local state representatives and reached out to them. While my neighborhood had both a state senator and house representative, I not only reached out to both of them, but also to representatives who I had

---

1. Ramey, Corinne, "Grown-Ups Fight for Children's Right to Sell Lukewarm Lemonade," (July 22, 2018) *The Wall Street Journal* online.

geographical connections to. In total, I reached out to about ten representatives, hoping someone would want to help.

It only took a few hours for my local state senate representative to respond and come to my house, sit on my living room couch, and agree to work with me. I shared with her that through my research, I discovered that Utah had recently passed a similar law, and my suggestion was that we should model Colorado's bill after Utah. On my couch, she got on her phone, called in a bill to get it documented — "Legalizing Minors' Businesses" — and we were off to the races.

We created a bipartisan bill. Democrats and Republicans alike could get behind the idea of supporting kids' businesses by reducing the bureaucratic barriers. This created a more equitable playing ground for all kids, and encouraged entrepreneurship, as well as the founding principles that this country was based upon.

We gathered support from throughout the state, from Scouts to youth groups to kids business clubs. Together, we created a kids' business at the state capital to generate support and local buzz. We contacted local businesses across the state who agreed to sponsor the bill.

And then, we testified.

My kids testified, along with many others. "Please help kids' business. We want to sell lemonade legally," my middle child said, in a room full of lawmakers and media.

Leadership Lemonade Lesson #5:
Challenge the status quo

Leaders shouldn't be afraid of proposing a new idea that may be worth pursuing, even if it hasn't been done before. If I had the attitude that the law is the law, then nothing would have changed.

Leadership Lemonade Lesson #6:
Lead with conviction and others follow

Conviction is believing so strongly in a firmly held belief or opinion. Great leaders have a strong sense of who they are and what they believe in. People are drawn to those

who have a clear sense of purpose and stand for what
they believe in.

About nine months after our lemonade stand was initially shut
down, kids' businesses became legal in the state of Colorado, without
all of the red tape! When we participated in the governor's bill signing,
a huge wave of relief flooded over me. We had done it!

Country Time Lemonade threw us a party in the same location
where the police had shut down my boys' lemonade stand. There were
jumpy houses, clowns, people face-painting kids, and unlimited glasses
of lemonade.

Since then, progress continues. States continue to pass legislation,
modifying kids' lemonade stand laws. In total, 18 states have changed
their laws around kids' lemonade stands since our movement began.

Adults can lead and make a difference, and so can kids. Whether we
are 5 or 50, we can all lead with positive impact, as we have the courage
to stand up for what we believe in, challenge the status quo, and follow
through with conviction.

About Nick Grubiša

Nikola Grubiša is a strategic advisor and mentor to founders, breakthrough performers, and first-class managers. Working with selected clients, including five national Fortune 10 enterprises, he creates personalized, custom-built systems for managing people and increasing productivity. He is the founder of EMMA (European Management Matrix), a unique leadership and productivity-boosting system that eliminates blind spots and gray areas in the workspace.

For more information regarding our authors, please visit our webpage!
BestSellerPublishing.org/ExpertLeadership

Chapter 3

Introducing "The European Management Matrix"

(or How I Told My $1.7 Billion Client That His Leadership Is Totally Off)

by Nick Grubiša

When you receive an SMS before sunrise, you never know what it might bring. Especially when it comes from a personal cell phone of a whale client.

But that day, I was in luck. The founder of the biggest private insurance company in the country sent me the latest report on his progress. He drastically improved some key performance indicators. "Thanks to your Management Matrix," he added.

I was happy for him. Not so much because of the results; I knew he would shine. After all, he is known as a king of sales. I was happy because he got The Matrix.

The Major Culprit Behind Many Leadership Failures

Two and a half years ago, when we started working together, the situation was not that nice. He was going through some difficulties, and we discussed working together, especially around conducting meetings and delegating tasks.

I asked him to record conversations with his key executives and send me the recordings. After listening to a few of them, the pattern became apparent. He was way too liberal. I spotted two things that stuck out like fried chicken on a vegan menu.

The first was his relationship with employees. He treated everyone alike: the successful, highly independent, and responsible superstars on one side and the underperforming ones on the other. He listened to their suggestions, aiming to accommodate them.

The second problem was related to the second group: underperformers. Their game was avoiding tasks and responsibilities in a very clever way. They continually suggested some improvements and upgrades and offered to work on them. The whole purpose was switching from measurable tasks to some muddy "working on it" assignments. It was just a diversion and a way to escape responsibility.

Well, I am a very straightforward person, and I always say what I mean, even if that could lead to losing the contract. I gasped for air and told the founder — very politely — that his leadership was off. I said, "You are a great visionary and decision-maker but not the best babysitter, aka manager."

He nodded. No drama, no excuses. After a few seconds, he asked three questions:

- Can you fix it?
- How long should it take, and what resources would we need?
- What should be done first?

That meant I was in.

We got to work. There were two major bottlenecks I suggested be resolved immediately.

THE EUROPEAN MANAGEMENT MATRIX: FIRST AID

First, I instructed him to check the first-line managers. These are supervisors who control the bottom-line performers. There are two main requirements for the first-line supervisors, in his case, the team leaders of the outbound callers:

- They should be great demonstrators
- They should be great coaches, which includes supervising and controlling

(Demanding these two requirements was my magic wand when I worked with national Fortune 10 companies. When we fixed the first-line management, many things came together quickly.)

Every manager was checked and tested in real-case scenarios by these requirements:

- Can they demonstrate how to call a customer and make an appointment, including resolving objections and taking a customer from "Who the heck are you?" to "Let's meet?"
- Can they transfer this knowledge to callers and maintain key performance indicators (KPIs) (activity, productivity, quality)?
- Can they spot shortcomings in employees and effectively resolve them?
- Can they prioritize the work and get consistent results from employees in all situations and circumstances?

"Above all, meeting one condition is a must," I told him. "At least one person in the company needs to perform the job well."

Three borderline situations are possible:

- If that person is a performer, they can serve as a demonstrator and base from which the company creates a systematic goal-getting approach and passes it on to others.
- If that person is a manager, they are responsible for creating a system, passing it on to subordinates, and getting results.
- If not even one person can consistently achieve the required results, rectifying that situation should be the absolute priority.

Second, I suggested the assignment of a clear responsibility to every employee. For example, some outbound callers didn't know what they were responsible for. When they received instructions from a manager but didn't perform well, whose fault was that? Was it theirs because they didn't listen or carry out a task as agreed? Or, was it the managers' fault because

- The callers weren't introduced to the task through a good demonstration?
- Or the callers didn't receive clear instructions?
- Or the callers weren't supervised effectively?

We assigned clear, measurable goals to everyone and made them responsible to meet them. Besides, their salary was exclusively results-based. The basis for the results was not the number of sales meetings they arranged but the revenue the agent generated from those meetings.

We also eradicated the "working on improving" diversion. One of the new rules was that the person proposing the "improving" is also responsible for completing the task and achieving better results than before. As expected, suggestions vanished overnight.

Clear and measurable goals that employees have already demonstrated they can achieve lead to straightforward expectations and transparent responsibility. Responsibility kills procrastination, excuses, excessive drama, and blaming others. Consequently, focus and priorities shift, and productivity increases.

After the changes, I told the founder his job was consolidating the new situation. "People will fight for the old circumstances and even sabotage new rules. That's natural. Just persist, gently but strictly. It should take around three to six months. After that, we will work on systematizing the process, checklists, and self-controlled jobs."

THE ESSENCE OF THE EUROPEAN MANAGEMENT MATRIX

The first-aid solution I offered the founder was taken directly from my secret weapon: The European Management Matrix (EMMA). It puts every employee in the proper perspective in terms of their boss, clarifies responsibilities, uncovers gray areas and bottlenecks, suggests practical solutions, and more.

EMMA consists of nine boxes (3×3). It is fractal by nature so can be used at all company levels.

THE EUROPEAN MANAGEMENT MATRIX (EMMA)

A1 Idea provider/ Skillful performer	**A2** Decision maker	**A3** Manager
B1 Artist	**B2** Expert	**B3** Organizer
C1 Independent goal-getter, committed and dedicated to results	**C2** Semi-independent achiever, responsible for their decisions and results	**C3** Diligent performer, responsible for following instructions

Superior / *Subordinate*

© Nikola Grubiša

The upper horizontal line holds boxes A1, A2, and A3. Implementing EMMA to the first person in the company, these boxes define the leader through functional added value and their three primary functions:

- A1: Idea provider/skillful performer
- A2: Decision-maker
- A3: Manager

Every business needs all three — the idea or skill the founder brings into the game, someone to make core decisions, and someone to lead/manage employees. The first step for a leader is to determine which description applies to them. Usually, an entrepreneur is a combination of A1 and A2.

In line A, a person can occupy one or two boxes but not all three. (Although the first reaction for entrepreneurs would be, "That's all me.")

Below line A is line B. It describes the same person but through the lenses of delegation and control over processes. The boxes are

- B1: Artist

- B2: Expert

- B3: Organizer

A person can occupy only one box in line B, considering one person — one task.

Artists do everything on their own. Not only are they irreplaceable, but they remain in control of everything. All decisions must be aligned with their ideas and expectations.

Among other problems, that kind of leadership kills inspiration, fresh ideas, and wisdom in coworkers. The whole system is set to support the leader's "smartest man in the room" thinking.

Can artists be successful? Yes, if they create one of the two specially designed environments that support their characters.

The B2 box is reserved for experts. They are willing to delegate some work but remain in control of the major activity. A typical example is car repair shop bosses who delegate all the tasks to employees, but restore the old-timers' engines themselves.

Experts are way ahead of artists because they have learned to trust employees.

Many leaders who reach that point gradually go all the way and become organizers (box B3). They are willing to leave responsibilities to others and trust them enough to take themselves out of the operations completely. They fill all positions with qualified people, allowing them to execute the work while the leaders themselves engage exclusively in making strategic decisions.

Below the first two lines that describe the superior, the EMMA's third line, C, is reserved for subordinates. It has three boxes that describe only three kinds of employees every company should have, according to their capabilities, character, and responsibilities:

- C1: Committed, independent, responsible, proactive employees. They take full responsibility for their tasks and goals and need no additional management. (Think of an agency you outsource some tasks to; these are that kind of people.)

- C2: Also powerful, independent, and responsible employees with self-initiative. They are not as inventive or maybe experienced as the first group, so they need little help. However, they still make decisions independently and take full responsibility for their work. Instructions for them come from the leader, but daily support comes from their manager. (Very important.)

- C3: Employees who don't want to make any decisions but follow the proven system. They need a demonstration of their work, detailed instructions, and a checklist. If the company doesn't have tasks systemized, C3 employees need the constant supervision of a first-line manager.

However, it is not about one of the groups being somehow better than the other. All of the employees, C1, C2, and C3, should

- have skills, abilities, sufficient experience, and competence to succeed at work
- be responsible for achieving assigned tasks and goals
- have suitable character, including values
- be willing/self-motivated to perform the tasks

A subordinate can occupy only one box for one task in line C.

After placing two persons in The Matrix, magic happens. Every box requires special treatment, and connections between superiors and subordinates have defined regulations. By knowing the rules and guidelines for all the boxes and affiliations, you get a blueprint for leadership. Here are some directions:

- The decision-maker (A2), who almost by the rule isn't a good manager, can lead only C1 employees successfully.

- An artist (B1) would want to work personally with employees C1, C2, and C3 (never a good idea).

- A manager (A3) can take two roles: an expert (B2) with employees who need demonstration (C3) and an organizer (B3) with others (C2). That's normal.

- Employees C2 and C3 need a manager.

- Etc.

HOW TO 10× SOME KPIS

The rules mentioned above are exactly what we implement with my client. We created the exact task for every employee, including middle management. They got a timetable that represented their workday hour by hour. It was a game-changer.

We defined the tipping points that served as red flags and how to protect the system: if the person hit one of the tipping points, scenario B was unveiled automatically.

The next thing we did was the founder's new role. "Since I am an idea provider and decision-maker," he concluded, "I must concentrate on my biggest contributions more and step away from dealing with too many people."

That was the biggest breakthrough for him. He thought he was good with people. He was, but only with a specific group of performers.

We prepared a full-circle checklist (FCC) for every employee. It goes like this: First, employees control themselves by ticking each completed task. Then, their manager controls whether employees have checked all tasks and randomly checks performance. On the third level, the manager's superior seeks deviations and connections between underperformance and checklists.

That way, the control process gets a new focus and higher purpose. It is no longer a bureaucratic task but a goal-directed and system-improving process.

We also follow the "Never twice" rule. Every problem should occur only once. Then, it is corrected and rooted out at its core, so it is impossible to manifest again.

The result? Despite the client's off-the-chart sales success from the past — he sold $1.7 billion worth of cheap products on a $2 million market (Slovenia, Europe), including up to $23 million a month — he improved some key performance indicators nearly tenfold.

He didn't believe it could even be possible. But I did. I witnessed it way too many times to be surprised. Now, a question for you. If even he could increase his results so much, what would redefining leadership bring to you?

ABOUT ANGELA SUTTON, PhD

What if the path to lasting business success is building relationships strong enough to earn deep buy-in from everyone who touches your product?

Angela Sutton, PhD, helps B2B founders and product managers scale by aligning internal teams and earning lasting customer commitment. As the author of *Sell Bigger: Unlock Repeat Business By Transforming How You Communicate*, she brings over 25 years of Silicon Valley experience in technical product management, product marketing, AI-driven process automation, and personalized customer engagement.

From automating chip design in the early internet era to leading eight-figure enterprise software, SaaS product lines, and consumer electronics teams, Angela turns complex solutions into systems that build trust, drive alignment, and power both team momentum and customer growth.

For more information regarding our authors,
please visit our webpage!
BestSellerPublishing.org/ExpertLeadership

CHAPTER 4

THE CONNECTION ADVANTAGE
(FOUR WAYS THAT LEADERS COMMUNICATE TO CONNECT ... AND HOW YOU CAN TOO)

BY ANGELA SUTTON, PHD

My career started at a research laboratory in Palo Alto, California, in the late 1980s.

It was a pivotal decade that saw the rise of the personal computer, all made possible by new high-performance semiconductors and micro-processors. Email became available to the general public thanks to the advent of wide-scale internet, also powered by semiconductors — semiconductor chips were mind-blowingly exciting to me. My head would spin with the pace that they were evolving.

And there was a problem: It took great expertise and many months to design these chips. And then, even more months to check that no mistakes had been made along the way before we manufactured them. Design and testing had become a massive bottleneck!

And so, I created software algorithms that automated the design process ... so you could design and then check your work with a computer instead of by hand.

The impact of creating algorithms that designed these chips — and had the smarts to make the chips "smaller" and "faster" — was staggering. Making smaller, faster chips quickly opened the doors to cheaper computers and the equipment that was powering the internet — I got to work!

My software algorithms were hard to explain to my parents — their confused looks were difficult to mask.

"That's wonderful, darling."

It was at that point that I learned an important lesson:

I needed to use words that related to *their* world. That made *them* care.

Words such as: *"My algorithms create small and fast chips quickly. This means that every family can afford a computer at home and can stay in touch by sending messages that get delivered in seconds."*

My journey from engineering geek to human-facing product leader who could "connect" had begun.

This chapter answers this question:

> ➢ **How can you, as a leader, *relate* your complicated products or services to your teams and customers ... using sentences that form *connection* ... so that these people are inspired to work with you and are motivated to buy?**

In the course of creating this chapter, I interviewed several CEOs and executives, and studied industry leaders that I view to be great communicators. Four principles emerged.

Please feel free to get out your pencil and use templates in this chapter in your business, as you read along.

Let's get started!

1. LEAD WITH QUESTIONS: "EMPATHY AND LISTENING ... BEFORE PROBLEM-SOLVING"

In Dale Carnegie's book *How to Win Friends and Influence People*, he says, "Make the other person feel important and do it sincerely."

Marc Benioff, the CEO of Salesforce, is known to have empathetically listened to two female employees about pay inequalities between male and female employees at the company. He showed his sincerity by initiating an audit that revealed their hypothesis to be true. He listened.

Questions for your business:

- How can asking the right questions in the right order improve a leader's effectiveness?

- How can you create an organizational culture that values problem understanding and connecting with others?

Consider this. A friend was struggling to use some new video editing software. We hopped on a video conference call where she could share her screen, and I asked her to show me the problem.

As I fixed a few settings to make everything work, I noticed that she wasn't herself. She was interjecting more complaints about the software. With everything working and ready to go, she became, surprisingly, even more upset, squinting and moving around uncomfortably on her seat.

The reason? I had fixed her problem without first showing empathy.

What does this have to do with how leaders communicate in business?

Leaders focus on opening doors to start a conversation — they empathize. They make the other person "feel heard" ... They do this *before* they fix a problem.

Here's a conversational "empathy first" sequence to use before you attempt to help solve a problem.

Repeat what the person said (their PROBLEM).
Ask if you got it right.
Empathize.
Ask for more details about why it matters.

> **Example:**
> **REPEAT AND CHECK:** *So you are saying that you are experiencing [PROBLEM] — is that correct?*
> **EMPATHIZE:** *Oh no — I know how that can be. I am so sorry.*
> **ASK FOR DETAILS:** *Could you tell me more about [PROBLEM]? What happened?*
> **ASK WHY IT MATTERS:** *Could you help me understand a bit more about why this is important?*

When you lead with questions that shows empathy, you will gain a deeper connection and understanding with the people that you lead.

2. MAKE THEM CARE ... WITH A STORY

Richard Branson, the founder of airline Virgin Atlantic, shares the story of how a canceled flight that left him stranded led him to charter a plane and sell tickets to fellow stranded passengers. This move sparked his idea to start an airline. Reed Hastings, co-founder of Netflix, became irritated by video rental store late fees. This drove him to start Netflix, a company that initially just shipped movie CDs through the mail, with no late fees. These origin stories give you a sense of what inspired these leaders.

For those of us with complex products to sell, a story can articulate a complex idea. Indeed, London School of Business's research revealed that people retain *65%–70% of information when conveyed through a story,* yet only *5%–10%* when the same information is conveyed via statistical data.

How much data is remembered?

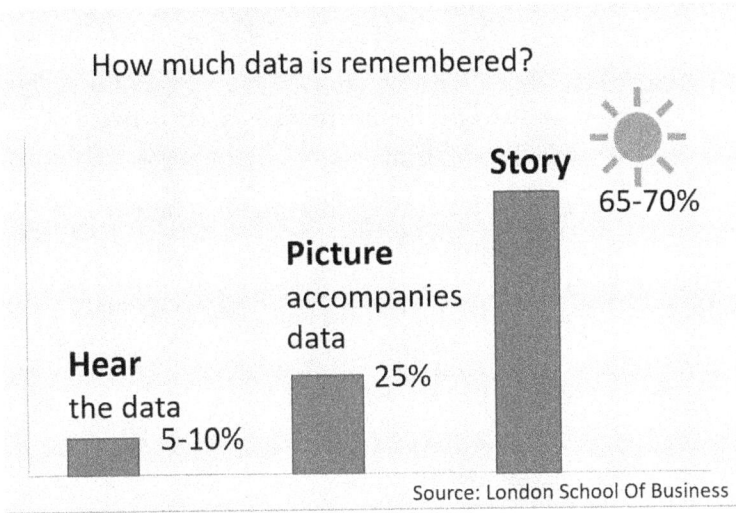

Source: London School Of Business

We can probably all relate.

A *story* about a hungry child in a Save the Children ad pulls us in to make us emotionally want to donate to the cause. A boring speech about how much it costs to feed each child would have been easily ignored.

In his book on leadership storytelling, Stephen Denning puts this very simply. Stories can convey values, goals, and vision in a way that facts and figures alone cannot.

How can you use stories in your business?

Many people get stuck, thinking … "No one's going to be interested in *my* personal stories." The exact opposite is true. I will show you exactly how everyday things that happen to you make *great* stories … Why? Because your audience has shared those very same experiences. All we need to do is link the story to what you planned to talk about. You can follow these two steps.

STEP 1: Jot down short story ideas.

1. A tense struggle, failure, roadblock, challenge, or everyday problem

2. Something that happened to you that taught you something

3. A "moment of enlightenment"/ a pivotal moment in your life

4. A funny thing that happened

5. A conversation you had with a customer that showcases how you care

STEP 2: Place your short story in front of your "main message," that is, the thing you wanted to talk about in your presentation/email or so on.

STEP 3: Link the story to your message with a one sentence transition phrase.

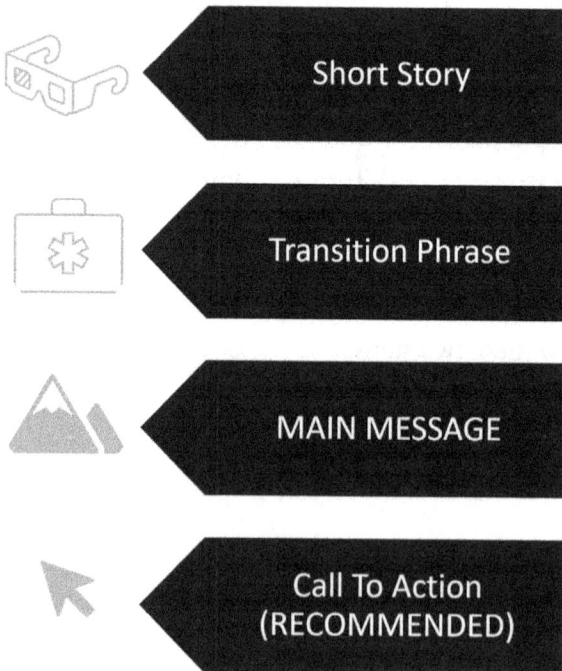

Short Story

Transition Phrase

MAIN MESSAGE

Call To Action
(RECOMMENDED)

Here's an example:

SHORT STORY	"Possible rain in the next hour"… It was dry and bright outside, so I figured I'd take my chances — I harnessed up the border collies, ready for our walk.
	About 10 minutes into the walk, I felt a spot of rain — no big deal … 15 minutes in, we had the chance to take a shorter route back as the clouds turned a little darker. … I decided to keep heading up the hill for our hour-long route. Twenty-five minutes in … the tap of continuous light rain … My skin increasingly wet but jacket holding up as the rain intensity seemed to slowly increase …
	If you've ever walked a border collie you know that they like to keep up a fast pace and that pace was keeping us super warm. Forty minutes in a massive downpour, I felt icicles of water seeping down my neck … Out of nowhere, the wind kicked up … I was suddenly shivering
TRANSITION PHRASE	What does this walk have to do with business?
MAIN MESSAGE	Well when you get a tiny bit wet and slowly a bit more wet until you suddenly realize that you are soaked, it's like that happens right before a customer unsubscribes from your service …
	They suffer a small amount for a while … The pain grows so slowly that they barely notice … Until one day, just like when the wind kicks up, something pushes them over the edge.
CALL TO ACTION	**How can we know that customers are at risk of leaving in time to do something about it?**
	Join our 1-hour workshop to find three actionable things that you can do.

This story framework is one of my favorites for emails and presentations.

I invite you to visit the anthology author page (see recurring link in About the Author sections) and click on the SellBigger link or read my book *Sell Bigger* to access additional storytelling frameworks that you can put to work in your business.

3. A MISSION AND VISION STATEMENT THAT PEOPLE CAN RALLY BEHIND

During a trip to Italy, Howard Schultz, the former CEO and Chairman of Starbucks, became inspired by the Italian coffee culture. He envisioned Starbucks as a place between work and home, where people could enjoy a sense of community and connection over a cup of coffee. By telling this very story, Schultz not only shaped the Starbucks vision of community but also cultivated a deep connection with employees and customers worldwide. And you can do the same.

Imagine for a minute that you have a software product that automates a factory's shipping process. You step into an elevator with Oprah Winfrey. She asks what you do for a living …

- What would you say to pique her interest? And …

- How can you craft words that appeal to her identity, her values, her experiences so that she would instantly rally behind you?

Answer: **Make your words about a purpose and benefit you *both* care about. That is, tell her your mission and vision.** Here's an example:

(VISION)	*I believe* in helping manufacturers run a headache-free business, one product, one business at a time
(MISSION) **I help . . .** **(Get) . . .** **So that they . . .** **Even if . . .** **You can find** **out more . . .**	small businesses with physical products create and ship them at scale, worry-free now feel they are in control of their revenue stream they don't think they have time to put new tools in place by watching a FREE webinar HERE

Here's a template for your Vision and Mission statement ...

(VISION)
I believe [FUTURE my customers want] / [PURPOSE] / [BIG IDEA] / [NEW WAY to solve problem]

(MISSION)
I help [WHO YOU SERVE]
Get [THING THEY WANT]

So that they can feel [BENEFIT] / avoid [FEAR]

Even if [COMMON EXCUSE OR OBJECTION FOR NOT USING YOUR SERVICE].
You can find out more here _____.

Short version:

Condensed Vision and Mission template
To give [BENEFIT] *to* [WHO YOU SERVE]
for [PURPOSE]

Now, grab a beverage of choice and create your mission and vision statement!

4. RESONATE WITH THEIR "WHY"

Under the leadership of Steve Jobs, Apple Inc. consistently communicated its core belief in challenging the status quo. This belief was evident in everything from the sleek look of their products and Steve's 2007 "reveal" of the first iPhone, to Apple's "Think Different" marketing campaign.

In its "Think Different" campaign, Apple was tapping into its customers' core beliefs and values …

to be creative, empowered, optimistic about the future, and feel a sense of individuality.

Our core beliefs and values are sometimes referred to as our "Why." This can be our deep passions, life purpose, and desire for impact and growth.

Simon Sinek is renowned for saying, "People don't buy what you do; they buy why you do it" and so, the question is this:

- How can you do what Apple did and resonate with your customer's "Why?"

Here are questions that leaders can ask to identify the "Why" of their team and customers:

Their Values:

    Impact: *"What legacy do you hope to leave in your professional or personal life?"*

Their Beliefs:

    Life purpose:

    "When have you felt most fulfilled or satisfied with your life, and why?"

    "Who do you want to be?"

    Passion: *"What do you love about what you do?"*

    Growth: *"Who has been the most influential person in your life, and why?"*

CONCLUSION

As leaders, we might ask:

- "What kind of relationship do we want to create with our team and customers?"
- "What doors can we open by connecting with them?"

We can connect, not by talking about our products but instead by using stories, by listening, by having a clear mission and a vision that people can rally behind … and by understanding and aligning with our team's and customer's "Why."

If you found the conversations and templates in this chapter helpful, drop me a line.

I'd love to connect !! angela@marketfastforward.com

Want to lead with connection?

Again, I invite you to visit the author webpage (see recurring link in About the Author sections) and click on the SellBigger link for more resources.

References

- *How to Win Friends and Influence People*, by Dale Carnegie
- *Pour Your Heart Into It: How Starbucks Built a Company One Cup at a Time*, by Howard Schultz
- *Start With Why: How Great Leaders Inspire Everyone to Take Action*, by Simon Sinek
- *Steve Jobs: A Biography*, by Walter Isaacson
- *The Leader's Guide to Storytelling: Mastering the Art and Discipline of Business Narrative*, by Stephen Denning
- *Sell Bigger: Unlock Repeat Business by Transforming How You Communicate*, by Angela Sutton, PhD

About Greg Mohr

Greg Mohr started off his work life in the restaurant industry. Later, climbing the corporate ladder, he worked in the semiconductor industry for about 15 years. During this time, he earned an MBA degree, specializing in management information systems.

As he loves sharing, Greg eventually found himself laid off, and it was a blessing. He saw an opportunity, and knew it was now or never. Working with a franchise consultant, Greg found a great fit after narrowing his goals and criteria. He never looked back. Today, he helps others find their way on the same path at Franchise Maven.

For more information regarding our authors,
please visit our webpage!
BestSellerPublishing.org/ExpertLeadership

CHAPTER 5

THE NEW FRANCHISE FRONTIER

(FIVE VALUES FOR TRAILBLAZING IN BUSINESS)

BY GREG MOHR

Every day, I have the privilege of working with individuals who defy convention and chart their own paths to success as franchise leaders in unexpected fields. From doctors to real estate investors, from fundraisers to business professionals, the diverse backgrounds and experiences of my clients highlight the remarkable versatility and adaptability of the franchise model. What unites them is a shared passion for entrepreneurship and a desire to make a meaningful impact in their chosen industries. Together, we navigate the intricate landscape of franchising, exploring opportunities that align with their unique skills, interests, and aspirations. In doing so, we challenge traditional notions of what it means to be a franchise leader, embracing innovation, creativity, and resilience as we carve out new territories and redefine success. Through their stories, we discover the transformative power of franchising to empower individuals to pursue their dreams and become leaders in unexpected fields.

VISION

When I was assisting Ben and Tricia in their quest to find the perfect franchise opportunity, Tricia remained mostly in the background, allowing Ben to take the lead. As real estate investors seeking to diversify their portfolio, they were initially drawn to semi-passive franchise options that could be managed by someone else. However, as they explored various franchise possibilities, Tricia's vision for their future took an unexpected turn.

Amidst their search, Tricia had a moment of clarity and conviction. She realized that the electrical services franchise they were considering had the potential to fulfill her own aspirations of leadership and hands-on involvement. Despite her lack of experience in the field, Tricia envisioned herself at the helm, leading a team of electricians, including a master electrician. This bold vision marked a significant departure from their initial plans of a semi-absentee ownership model.

Tricia's newfound vision sparked a transformation in their approach to the franchise business. With her at the forefront, they shifted gears and embraced a more hands-on role in the operation of the business. Despite the uncertainties and challenges that lay ahead, Tricia's unwavering belief in her ability to lead and succeed propelled them forward.

Now, Ben and Tricia are on the brink of embarking on a new chapter as rookies of the year in their chosen franchise. Tricia's vision, coupled with their shared determination and dedication, has set them on a path toward achieving their goals and realizing their dreams in the franchise industry.

Tricia's story illustrates the transformative power of vision in guiding individuals toward unexpected opportunities and uncharted territories. Her ability to envision herself in a leadership role not only altered the trajectory of their franchise journey but also paved the way for personal and professional growth. In the world of franchising, a clear and compelling vision can serve as a catalyst for success, empowering individuals to chart their own course and turn their dreams into reality.

COMMUNICATION

When Nourhen reached out to me on LinkedIn, I was immediately struck by her exceptional ability to communicate her goals and aspirations, despite English being her second language. Living in Germany at the time, Nourhen expressed her desire to relocate to San Diego and embark on a new chapter in her career. Her clarity and articulateness left a lasting impression on me.

Having worked with business professionals in Germany, Nourhen possessed a wealth of experience and expertise that she was eager to leverage in her new venture in the United States. She articulated her vision of wanting to support other businesspeople in the U.S. with a level of clarity and conviction that was truly impressive.

Together, we identified a business development franchise as the perfect opportunity for Nourhen to channel her passion and expertise. It was a bold move, requiring her to take a chance on herself and step out of her comfort zone. However, Nourhen's superlative communication skills and unwavering determination made her more than capable of rising to the challenge.

Starting a business in a new country and convincing other businesspeople of your value proposition requires not only courage but also exceptional communication skills. Nourhen's ability to effectively convey her expertise and value proposition played a crucial role in her success. She understood the importance of clear and persuasive communication in building trust and credibility with potential clients and partners.

Nourhen's journey serves as a powerful reminder of the transformative impact of effective communication in the world of business. Whether it's conveying your vision, persuading stakeholders, or building relationships, strong communication skills are essential for success. Nourhen's ability to communicate with clarity and confidence not only enabled her to overcome obstacles but also positioned her for success in her new venture in San Diego.

RESILIENCE

When Ryan approached me, he was working in fundraising, juggling a demanding job that required extensive travel — a lifestyle that left him longing for more time with his young family. Determined to prioritize family time, Ryan set his sights on running a business that would afford him the flexibility to be present for his loved ones, especially in the evenings and on weekends. However, he also harbored a long-term vision of eventually stepping back from the day-to-day operations to devote even more time to his family.

Ryan understood that achieving this delicate balance between work and family would require resilience and unwavering commitment. Despite the challenges and uncertainties that lay ahead, he was determined to see his vision through to fruition. With grit and determination, Ryan embarked on a journey of entrepreneurship, building his kitchen remodeling franchise from the ground up over the course of three years.

The road to success was not without its obstacles. Ryan encountered setbacks and challenges along the way, from navigating the complexities of the business world to managing the demands of family life. However, his resilience and perseverance enabled him to overcome each hurdle, emerging stronger and more determined than before.

After three years of hard work and dedication, Ryan successfully sold his kitchen remodeling franchise for a significant profit — a testament to his resilience and business acumen. Undeterred by the challenges of entrepreneurship, he ventured into a new business opportunity: a kids' trampoline park franchise. With careful planning and foresight, Ryan has managed to streamline operations to the point where he now runs the business almost entirely absentee, allowing him to prioritize his family while still enjoying the benefits of business ownership.

Ryan's journey exemplifies the power of resilience in overcoming obstacles and achieving success. Through his unwavering determination and perseverance, he has transformed his vision of work-life balance into a reality, proving that with resilience as a guiding force, anything is possible.

EMPATHY

As Jim and I delved into the world of franchise opportunities, it became apparent that his interest lay in essential home services — businesses resilient enough to weather economic fluctuations and ideally semi-passive in nature. However, as our conversations deepened, another aspect of Jim's character emerged: his deep-seated empathy for seniors and his desire to make a difference in their lives.

Despite the availability of senior care franchises in his area, the requirement for full-time involvement posed a significant hurdle for Jim, who had a strong sense of empathy toward seniors but also needed a business that allowed for flexibility. However, driven by his passion for helping others, particularly seniors, Jim made the courageous decision to pursue his dream and take a leap of faith.

For Jim, stepping away from his job to commit fully to the senior care franchise was not just a career move — it was a profound expression of empathy and compassion. With a wife and two children to support, this decision carried immense weight and risk. However, Jim's empathy for seniors and his unwavering commitment to making a positive impact in their lives outweighed the uncertainties and challenges he faced.

By choosing to prioritize empathy and pursue his passion for helping seniors, Jim embarked on a journey of both personal and professional growth. He understood that success in the franchise business would require not only financial investment but also emotional investment — a genuine commitment to understanding and meeting the needs of seniors in his community.

Through thorough investigation and careful consideration of the franchise opportunity, Jim took a chance on himself and his dream of making a difference in the lives of seniors. His journey serves as a testament to the transformative power of empathy, demonstrating how compassion and understanding can drive individuals to overcome obstacles and pursue their true calling in life.

INTEGRITY

Jay, a dedicated doctor with a passion for helping underprivileged individuals access healthcare, embarked on a mission to make a difference in the lives of those in need. His vision was not only to provide quality healthcare services but also to create sustainable support systems for underserved communities. With unwavering integrity as his guiding principle, Jay envisioned building a network of franchises that would not only generate profits but also contribute significantly to his cause of helping others.

As Jay and his team embarked on the journey of expanding his business portfolio, he remained transparent and forthcoming about his intentions. He made it clear to everyone involved that a substantial portion of the profits generated from the franchises would be directed toward providing healthcare services to underprivileged individuals.

This commitment to transparency and integrity earned Jay the trust and admiration of his team members, who were inspired by his selfless dedication to making a positive impact in the world.

Through Jay's steadfast leadership and unwavering commitment to integrity, his empire of franchises grew steadily. From humble beginnings, they expanded to include a network of 85 hair salons, each contributing to the greater mission of supporting underprivileged communities with healthcare services. For Jay, who had never undertaken anything of this magnitude before, it was a testament to the power of integrity and dedication to a noble cause.

Jay's story exemplifies the profound impact that integrity can have on both business success and social responsibility. By staying true to his values and remaining transparent about his intentions, Jay not only built a successful business empire but also made a meaningful difference in the lives of countless individuals. His unwavering commitment to integrity serves as an inspiration to others, demonstrating that with integrity as their compass, they too can achieve remarkable feats and create positive change in the world.

CONCLUSION

Witnessing the transformation of individuals as they evolve into confident and successful franchise leaders is truly inspiring. Each success story serves as a testament to the power of determination, resilience, and self-belief. As I reflect on the journeys of my clients, I am reminded of the endless possibilities that await those who dare to take a chance on themselves. I encourage readers to embrace their aspirations, step out of their comfort zones, and pursue their dreams with unwavering determination. Whether it's starting a new business venture, pursuing a passion project, or embarking on a journey of self-discovery, taking that first step toward personal and professional growth can be daunting. However, it is often in those moments of uncertainty and risk that we find our greatest opportunities for success and fulfillment. So, I urge you to seize the moment, trust in your abilities, and dare to become the architect of your own destiny. Your journey toward greatness begins with a single step — take a chance on yourself and watch as your dreams take flight.

For more information regarding our authors,
please visit our webpage!
BestSellerPublishing.org/ExpertLeadership

About Sharise M. Bijou, MSA, MSW, LCSW

Sharise M Bijou is a licensed clinical social worker almost 20 years of professional work experience. She also has a doctorate in philosophy with the focus being on leadership. She has served in the military as an officer for 16 years in mental health. She combines her leadership and training as a therapist to help others reach their optimal self.

For more information regarding our authors,
please visit our webpage!
BestSellerPublishing.org/ExpertLeadership

CHAPTER 6

TRUE LEADERSHIP
(A JOURNEY SHAPED BY EXPERIENCE)

BY SHARISE M. BIJOU, MSA, MSW, LCSW

The question of whether leadership is innate or acquired has long been a topic of debate. From a comprehensive perspective, life's trials, particularly personal traumas, can profoundly shape an individual's leadership abilities, allowing them to serve others effectively. Understanding how experiences can mold someone into a leader provides valuable insights into the nature of leadership.

Leadership is not merely about holding a position of authority or being the boss. It is about guiding individuals to achieve a goal. True leadership involves understanding people, knowing when to lead and when to follow, and fostering team growth while meeting deadlines and achieving positive outcomes, even in challenging situations. Creating an environment where a team can thrive is at the heart of effective leadership.

Many people believe that a college degree is essential for good leadership. However, life experiences can provide the wisdom, skills, and resilience necessary for leadership. For instance, consider the story of an individual who, as a 20-year-old high school dropout with a GED, took on significant leadership roles.

After giving birth at 17, she wasn't allowed to finish high school. Determined to continue her education, she earned her high school diploma at a community college, sneaking out of the house when her mother left for work. Soon after, she began working as a dispatcher for a multimillion-dollar ambulance company that also handled 9-1-1 calls. Within a year, she was promoted to the company's first female supervisor. This rapid ascent wasn't due to formal education but rather the skills and resilience developed through life's challenges.

The true impact of her leadership style became evident five years later, when her mother had a heart attack. Her mother called 9-1-1, and due to her location and lack of insurance, she was being taken to the nearest county hospital. However, one of the paramedics recognized her last name and asked if she knew a particular supervisor. Upon learning that she was the mother of this supervisor, the paramedic decided to take her to Loma Linda, California's top hospital for cardiology, saying, "She is not going to County, she is going to Loma Linda because [Monica] was the best supervisor I ever had." This decision saved her mother's life, highlighting how leadership had tangible, life-saving impacts, extending beyond the workplace.

Personal trauma, such as childhood abuse, can heighten an individual's awareness, allowing them to be more attuned to their colleagues' needs. Instead of fostering mistrust, this awareness can be used to become more discerning and supportive, showing empathy and providing assistance when necessary. This sensitivity can prove invaluable in creating a supportive work environment.

Setting boundaries is also crucial in leadership. Boundaries prevent favoritism, promote consistency, and ensure fairness, creating an environment of trust and safety. For example, after giving birth to her daughter, this individual was determined to protect her from the abuse she herself had endured. She set strict boundaries, prioritizing time with her daughter and preventing interruptions from others. This practice of setting boundaries carried over into her professional life, helping to create a fair and respectful work environment.

Clear, concise, and consistent communication is vital for effective leadership. It fosters competency, confidence, and teamwork. A mentor once shared that true leadership is when someone can fill your shoes in your absence. Keeping the team informed and engaged ensures they are well-prepared and confident in their roles. Feedback is essential for growth and improvement and should be a two-way street, used for both correcting and encouraging behavior. Honest feedback builds trust and helps employees feel supported and valued. This leader always told those she led, "I have your back; however, I will always hold you account-able." This approach ensured her team knew her expectations and felt supported.

Leading from the middle allows a leader to see everything and be more approachable. It fosters inclusivity and reduces favoritism, enabling leaders to notice and support even the most introverted team members. Leading from the middle involves getting out from behind the desk, routinely speaking to the team, and asking how they are doing. This approach helps gauge office morale firsthand and fosters a sense of support and approachability among the team.

Mentorship is another crucial aspect of leadership. A good mentor teaches with humility and honesty, helping others grow and develop. Surrounding oneself with inspiring people who push one to grow is vital for continuous personal and professional development. This leader had mentors who guided her through childhood trauma, and she sought to pour into others what had been poured into her.

Listening with the intent to understand is key. Observing, asking questions, and involving the team in decision-making processes helps build trust and ensures that everyone feels heard and valued. When changes are warranted, discussing recommendations with the team and receiving input from those who will execute the changes is important. This inclusive approach reduces resistance to change and fosters a collaborative environment.

Transparency in leadership fosters trust and reduces workplace stress. Being open and honest about thoughts and feelings creates a supportive and collaborative environment. A transparent leader elimi-nates competition and fosters teamwork, reducing overall stress. When a leader walks out of a room and another person can fill her shoes, that leader has done an excellent job.

Allowing experiences and challenges to fuel growth enables the creation of a workplace environment of empowerment and happiness. As Maya Angelou said, "People will forget what you said, people will forget what you did, but people will never forget how you made them feel." Effective leadership leaves a lasting impact on those you lead, shaping not just their professional lives but their personal ones as well.

Through embracing and overcoming personal adversities, the essence of leadership lies in empathy, communication, and the willingness to support and uplift others. This journey of growth and self-discovery continues to guide a leader's path, making them more resilient, understanding, and effective.

One of the most impactful lessons in leadership is the importance of resilience. Resilience is the ability to bounce back from adversity, and it is a cornerstone of leadership philosophy. Early life marked by challenges and hardships teaches the value of resilience. Every setback becomes an opportunity for growth, and maintaining a positive attitude in the face of adversity is crucial. Resilience is not only helpful in personal life but also a valuable asset in a professional career.

As a leader, resilience means staying calm and composed during crises, maintaining a forward-thinking mindset, and encouraging the team to persevere through tough times. It's about being a source of stability and inspiration for the team, showing them that challenges can be overcome with determination and a positive attitude. Sharing personal experiences of overcoming adversity can help motivate and inspire the team, fostering a culture of resilience and perseverance.

Empathy is another critical component of effective leadership. Empathy is the ability to understand and share the feelings of others. Personal experiences often give leaders a deep sense of empathy, which they use to connect with their team on a personal level. By showing empathy, leaders can build strong relationships with their team members, understand their needs and concerns, and provide the support the team needs to succeed.

Empathy also plays a crucial role in conflict resolution. In any workplace, conflicts are inevitable, but as a leader, it's important to handle them with empathy and understanding. By listening to all sides of a conflict, acknowledging the feelings of those involved, and working toward a fair resolution, a leader can help maintain a positive and harmonious work environment. Empathy not only helps resolve conflicts but also prevents them from escalating.

Continuous learning and personal development are also essential aspects of leadership. Leadership is not a destination but a journey of continuous growth and improvement. Leaders should always seek opportunities to learn and develop their skills, whether through formal education, professional training, or personal experiences. This commitment to continuous learning is instrumental in the success of a leader.

Seeking feedback from the team is a powerful tool for personal and professional development. Feedback helps leaders understand their strengths and areas for improvement and provides valuable insights into how they can better support their team. Creating an open and trusting environment where team members feel comfortable sharing their thoughts and opinions is crucial for effective feedback.

Mentorship is another key element of leadership. Throughout a leader's career, having mentors who provide guidance and support is invaluable. These mentors help the leader grow and develop, and the leader can pay it forward by mentoring others. Mentorship involves sharing knowledge, providing guidance, and helping others reach their full potential. It's about being a source of support and inspiration for those on their own leadership journey.

In conclusion, leadership is not just about holding a position of authority or being the boss. It's about guiding and supporting others, fostering a positive and inclusive work environment, and continuously growing and developing as a leader. Personal experiences shape leadership style and teach valuable lessons about resilience, empathy, continuous learning, and mentorship. By embracing these principles, leaders can create a workplace environment where their team can thrive and achieve their full potential.

About Neil Gordon

Neil Gordon is the author of *The Most Powerful Sentence of All Time.* He is a persuasion expert and messaging strategist who has helped countless thought leaders refine their ideas and amplify their impact. A former editor with Dutton, now a division of Penguin Random House, Neil has worked with *New York Times* best-selling authors and collaborated with major publishing houses such as Penguin Random House, HarperCollins, and Hay House. His writing and insights have been featured in *Forbes, Inc., Fortune, Entrepreneur,* and *Startups* magazine, as well as on TV networks like NBC and Fox.

For more information regarding our authors, please visit our webpage!
BestSellerPublishing.org/ExpertLeadership

CHAPTER 7

THE SILVER BULLET IN LEADERSHIP

(HOW PROFESSIONALS OFTEN MISS THE IMPORTANCE OF CONTEXT)

BY NEIL GORDON

[DISCLAIMER: This chapter references sexual violence.]

My client Alissa had the potential to impact thousands through her work.

However, one wouldn't know it from how her career had taken shape by 2018.

When I first began working with her, she was a college professor with expertise in sexual violence and criminal justice. She helped her students explore a different way of preventing the sexual violence that takes place every year.

With such complex and challenging subject matter, one would think that reaching people on an emotionally significant level would be a given. And while her students were fond of her and her department supported her work, her sense was that there was a much greater opportunity for her expertise to impact the world. She felt there wasn't a compelling connection between sexual violence and her own story.

This is because, quite unfortunately, Alissa was a victim of sexual violence herself.

When she was 16, Alissa was raped.

Yet, despite the intensity and fraught nature of her past, when she attempted to incorporate her story into her content, the result was what she describes as "very vanilla." She merely just stated a series of events as if she was listing the minutes of a board meeting.

What's more, she didn't just teach about sexual violence. She sought to share a whole different paradigm for relating to it — something known as restorative justice. She saw opportunities within the pursuit of restorative justice to help organizations reform how they responded to sexual violence and ultimately lessened the incidence of such horrors taking place.

In her words, she believed that "there's something bigger here that could benefit people."

She wanted greater momentum because she wanted to help save lives, and yet when we met, she was stalled in finding it.

Within a couple of years of our first meeting, however, things were very different. She had given a TEDx talk and written several books. Whereas before, she had needed to apply to speak at conferences, she was now receiving so many invitations, she had to pick and choose the gigs she wanted to accept. And she received several organizational and institutional contracts in the both the public and private sector.

In other words, she had found the momentum she sought.

While giving the TEDx talk and writing the books all contributed to this momentum, at the heart of Alissa's transformation was a single ingredient that made everything else possible. It's an ingredient that helped her integrate her expertise with her own story and take radical ownership of the contribution she's meant to make in the world.

And this ingredient forms the basis of this chapter.

THE THOUGHT LEADER'S STRUGGLE

Alissa's struggle was similar to that faced by many people I've helped. Each of them held a vision that could greatly benefit humanity, yet they inspired very few others to believe in that vision.

We can call Alissa and others like her a "thought leader," one who has formulated a different way to solve a meaningful problem and whose insight could greatly benefit society.

Alissa and everyone else had a persuasion problem. If most people have solved a problem one way over time, they likely fear trying something new. To be an impactful thought leader is to successfully convince others to try something different.

As of this writing, I've served many thousands of thought leaders. And what I find most amazing is that *every single person* with whom I've engaged in some aspect of my work falls prey to the same tragic mistake.

Each of them bombards people with information. Each of them is guilty of what I call the "show-up-and-throw-up."

Let's say someone is to give a talk. If they use the show-up-and-throw-up approach, they will spend their time on stage bombarding the audience with steps, tips, or concepts. I once saw a famous influencer give a keynote in which he outlined six concepts for being a successful entrepreneur. His whole talk was comprised of giving equal time to each of these concepts.

In Alissa's case, she would not only provide her audiences with a lot of information, but she would treat the fraught nature of sexual violence as merely factual.

It's understandable why experts like Alissa and the famous influencer approach their messaging in this way. Experts by their nature see problems through a highly specialized lens. They've gained a tremendous amount of knowledge and want to share that knowledge with others. Each of us who knows a lot want to connect with others through the lens of that experience. It helps us to feel seen and valued.

But in the Digital Age, we already have access to information. People don't need more information to get on board with a different way of doing things.

They need something else.

And there is a far more effective way to lead others toward the vision we wish to share.

THE INGREDIENT

You may be familiar with the movie *Moneyball*. In it, Brad Pitt plays the general manager of the Oakland A's baseball team in the early 2000s. The A's emerge as division leader, winning a record-breaking 20 games in a row.

The movie implies they achieved this because of the different way they filled their roster. Pitt is helped throughout the movie by a fictional character played by Jonah Hill. Early in the movie, Hill explains to Pitt the concept we now know as Moneyball.

He describes a failure among baseball's leaders to understand how to win. He states that most teams think in terms of buying players but they must think in terms of buying runs.

We can look at Hill as representing a thought leader needing to solve the persuasion problem — he has a different kind of solution and is setting out to convince others of its viability. However, it is the way that he does it in this scene that holds so much value to us.

For his part, Hill doesn't deluge Pitt with information. He instead distills everything down to a single, game-changing idea: the key to winning at baseball is not to buy players but rather to buy runs. This sentence is an example of what gave Alissa that momentum and has similarly served many thought leaders for thousands of years.

For example, let's look at the iconic work *The Art of War* by ancient Chinese military strategist Sun Tzu. Early in the first chapter, he is arguably guilty of show-up-and-throw-up when he writes about "five constant factors to be taken into account in one's deliberations" and other various frameworks. But then, on line 18 of the first chapter, he writes something else:

"All of warfare is based on deception."

Sun Tzu did what Hill did, which was to distill his expertise down to one, secret-sauce-like sentence.

More importantly, however, it's what I helped Alissa find that led to the momentum that followed. At the heart of her work was the sentence, "Healing from intimate harm requires connection."

I call this technique a "silver bullet." In monster lore, a silver bullet is the one thing that can kill werewolves. In our noisy world, this sentence is the one thing that can cut through and change everything for those who hear it.

A silver bullet is a thought leader's secret sauce. It's their recipe for the change they wish to see. Nearly every one of the most-viewed TED talks has a similarly distilled idea at the heart of their talk, and it shows up in best-selling nonfiction books as well.

The silver bullet is a cause-and-effect sentence, in that it is comprised of one action that leads to one outcome. When you buy runs, you win at baseball. When you deceive your opponent, you win at war. When you connect with those harmed in intimate ways, they can heal.

This one-to-one formula both gives the audience member the one thing they need to do next and the reason why they need to do it. But because they get this information all at once, it instantly empowers them.

One time, Alissa was working on a large contract, and a document was produced that introduced her and others as the facilitators of that engagement. One woman saw the letter and looked up Alissa's work. She watched her TEDx talk and reached out immediately. This was the first thing she said when they began their call:

> "This notion," she told Alissa, "that healing is linked to connection is so powerful I had to have a conversation with you."

One of my favorite things to do when I read a popular nonfiction book on my Kindle is to see if the most-highlighted passage in the book is a silver bullet. Usually it is, and thousands highlight it because of the same reason Alissa's silver bullet compelled the woman to reach out. In all these cases, they were suddenly empowered.

Those who do the show-up-and-throw-up falsely believe that it is information that empowers others. But it is really because they suddenly believe that change is possible.

Indeed, people are empowered not by that which they know is true but rather that which they believe is possible.

This is why Alissa got a TEDx talk and was offered contracts and everything else. Her audience didn't just learn about restorative justice. They believed it could help.

CREATING CONTEXT

It's important to recognize that Alissa didn't stand on the red dot at her TEDx event, say "Healing from intimate harm requires connection," and then stand there for the remaining 13 minutes she was on stage. Even though it empowers without context, we still benefit from offering context in the form of a strategically crafted talk, business proposal, or something else.

Consider the silver bullet of this chapter — that "people are empowered not by that which they know is true but rather that which they believe is possible." I didn't start this chapter with that sentence, nor is it the chapter's title. A silver bullet is not a tag line. In a talk, it's more likely to be placed in the second half as a climactic moment.

More than that, however, Alissa's silver bullet informed the decisions that went into the creation of her content. It guided her to integrate the raw, difficult nature of her story as a rape survivor with the concept of restorative justice. The clarity around one's silver bullet empowers the audience but it also does something else arguably more important — it empowers us.

While finding your silver bullet can take shape in many ways, there's a simple exercise you can try as inspired by *Moneyball*. Hill talks about people's failure to understand what's happening in baseball, and so your task is to think about the failure that others in your field perpetuate through false solutions. This is because contrast creates clarity, and contrasting our own solutions with those we least approve of can help us zero in on the essence of our work.

Consider the following fill-in-the-blank exercise:

> The failure in how (people) (solve problem) is that they (false solution). But the real way to (solve problem) is (true solution).

> Using the *Moneyball* example, we might write:

> The failure in how (team owners) (attempt to win) is that they (buy players). But the real way to (win) is to (buy runs).

This then leads us to one of many possible formats for a silver bullet:

The key to winning at baseball is not to buy players but rather to buy runs.

While there are many ways to format a silver bullet, this quick contrast exercise can get you started.

* * * *

If you struggle to persuade others of your vision's value, I call upon you to honor the distilled essence of that vision.

Yes, it will lead to more speaking opportunities, books, and contracts, and it will create a great deal of momentum for your thought leadership. But something even more important will take place because of this clarity.

For, once armed with your silver bullet, you will take radical ownership of the impact you're meant to have on the world.

About Rachael Draper, PhD

Dr. Draper, a translational cancer research professor with multiple patents, is currently working on two active INDs, bringing scientific rigor to everything she creates. After overcoming eating and alcohol use disorders, she continued to struggle with social anxiety and procrastination — until she found a way to rewire her brain. She developed the SOS Button App she will be discussing at the summit to help other lifelong strugglers of anxiety and depression regulate their nervous systems, break cycles of overwhelm, and regain control in minutes.

For more information regarding our authors,
please visit our webpage!
BestSellerPublishing.org/ExpertLeadership

CHAPTER 8

SELF-LEADERSHIP

(HARNESSING INNER SAFETY TO TAKE THE LEAD IN YOUR OWN LIFE)

BY RACHAEL DRAPER, PHD

Joanne, a successful 36-year-old software engineer living in Boulder, had been secretly battling bulimia since she was 12. She was married to a musician, and they had two children together. Joanne spent most of her day in front of a computer screen, coding and debugging software.

Her work, although intellectually stimulating, required little to no human interaction. This isolation was not limited to her professional life. Her marriage was deeply lonely, with both Joanne and her husband living in their own worlds, unable to connect with each other. Physical touch was a thing of the past, exacerbated by Joanne's unrelenting body-image insecurities.

One day, Joanne's husband confronted her with hidden camera footage taken from their bathroom showing evidence of her bulimia. The shame of being caught, and the exasperation of having already tried formal therapy, filled Joanne with such rage that she stormed out into the freezing woods surrounding their home without so much as grabbing a jacket. Joanne was a strong woman — a former pro-cyclist — and her husband was no match for her endurance.

She hid out in the woods for two hours, her body hot with rage. When she finally returned home, the tension between them was palpable. Over the coming weeks, they only spoke about required co-parenting logistics.

A Silent Scream

Joanne's eating disorder is not unique, but bulimia is often cloaked in secrecy and shame. It is a silent scream, a hidden battle fought behind closed doors. Once the bulimic pits food against the thinness ideal "required" for relational acceptance, two survival instincts — food and connection — are battling each other. Food is no longer safe because it deprives them of love. Relationships are not safe because they "require" thinness, which in turn requires food deprivation.

With no more safety available, the only other options are anxiety or depression. The bulimic tends to choose anxiety. Bulimia has been on a steady rise since 1970, with the most recent surge documented after the COVID-19 pandemic. "Unlike anorexia nervosa, for which a rich history has been traced to the Middle Ages, bulimia nervosa seems to have burst from the blue upon modern society and it has achieved widespread adoption in a very short period of time," says Dr. Albert Stunkard, a psychiatrist at the University of Pennsylvania.[2]

The bulimia "pandemic" has been attributed to two features of modern society: an abundance of processed sugar and high stress levels from a variety of sources. These sources include intergenerational trauma, childhood adverse experiences, social isolation, negative news cycles, social media, and even diversity, equity, and inclusion movements. Societal shifts, although empowering, also bring new challenges, as evidenced by the rise of addictions among women.

This trend is perhaps not surprising given a 2016 study published in the journal *Neuron* that found that stress activates addiction circuitry in the brain. Take the case of Betty Friedan, a leading figure in the feminist movement and author of *The Feminine Mystique*. In her book, she highlighted the dissatisfaction and unfulfillment many housewives felt, leading to a surge of women seeking employment. However, Friedan herself struggled with addiction to alcohol and prescription drugs, a struggle she attributed to the pressures of balancing work, family, and societal expectations. Today, both men and women are increasingly pressured to balance career and family workloads. Both genders have

---

2. Stunkard, A., "A description of eating disorders in 1932." *Am J Psychiatry*, 1990; 147:263–8.

had to enhance their ability to move flexibly between roles that were once traditionally masculine and feminine.

RISK, REWARD, AND BEHAVIOR

The struggle for safety extends far beyond eating disorders. According to the World Health Organization (WHO) and the International Labour Organization (ILO), depression and anxiety disorders result in the loss of approximately 12 billion working days annually, costing the global economy over $1 trillion each year.[3] The chronic stress of modern living can disrupt the normal development of the orbitofrontal cortex — a key player in the brain's decision-making process. This region of the brain is responsible for evaluating risks and rewards, and it plays a significant role in how we perceive ourselves and our willingness to engage socially. This may explain why, despite Joanne's incredible success, she still struggled with feelings of self-doubt and inadequacy. This is a common phenomenon among high achievers, often referred to as "impostor syndrome."

How does one change self-sabotaging behaviors? What about when the behaviors have unconscious drivers and changing them requires growth, discomfort, and risk? Other behaviors in this category include procrastination, insecure relational attachment, introversion, fear of public speaking, other eating disorders, and shopping or substance addictions. The leading evidence-based treatments for not just bulimia, but also for general anxiety, are cognitive behavioral therapy (CBT) and Prozac.

At its core, CBT refers to a family of techniques that promote more adaptive thinking and behaviors to alleviate distressing emotions like anxiety. Prozac regulates post-stress neuroinflammation and serotonergic signaling. However, it is estimated that 60% of those who receive first-line treatment for bulimia nervosa remain symptomatic.[4,5] Current

---

3. Bie, F., Yan, X., Xing, J., Wang, L., Xu, Y., Wang, G., Wang, Q., Guo, J., Qiao, J., Rao, Z., "Rising global burden of anxiety disorders among adolescents and young adults: trends, risk factors, and the impact of socioeconomic disparities and COVID-19 from 1990 to 2021." *Front Psychiatry*. November 26, 2024;15:1489427. doi: 10.3389/fpsyt.2024.1489427. PMID: 39691785; PMCID: PMC11651023.

4. Porges, Stephen, "Safety IS the Treatment." YouTube, uploaded by The Embody Lab, December 6, 2020.

5. Porges, S. W., "Polyvagal Theory: A Science of Safety." *Front Integr Neurosci.*, May 10, 2022; 16:871227. doi: 10.3389/fnint.2022.871227. PMID: 35645742; PMCID: PMC9131189.

options are clearly suboptimal not just for bulimics, but perhaps for everyone else with anxiety too.

"SAFETY IS THE TREATMENT"

Joanne's failure to respond to traditional anti-anxiety therapies is not unique. For Joanne, access to both CBT and Prozac required an embarrassing admission of her behavior to someone who usually has never been bulimic. Often, therapists, although highly educated and well-intentioned, also carry heavy student-debt loads and must charge around $200/hour and work at under-resourced facilities according to schedules that quickly burn them out. On top of that, there's the insurance paperwork if Joanne is lucky enough to be approved. Therapists would recommend "long-term" treatment, given that current statistics show 55% of people never fully recover from bulimia.[6,7]

In addition to the CBT framework, Joanne's therapists would rely on the "safety of the therapeutic relationship." The therapist will establish safety and trust by providing Joanne validation as she trudges through memories of her darkest moments. Let's say Joanne *still* feels stressed out and triggered, even after her "rent-a-friend" expertly shows her how her thoughts may be influencing her behaviors, the potential source of those thoughts, and that perhaps she could choose alternative thoughts. If so, another recourse could be a residential program away from her family where her ingestion, elimination, exertion, and weight are monitored and controlled.

Dr. Stephen Porges has said, "Safety is the treatment."[8] It is logical that if the inner anxiety one feels about having unfulfilled basic human needs is the root cause of being stuck in self-sabotaging behaviors, establishing an inner sense of safety while working toward meeting those needs should be the treatment goal.

---

6. Porges, Stephen, "Safety IS the Treatment." YouTube, uploaded by The Embody Lab, December 6, 2020.

7. Porges, S. W., "Polyvagal Theory: A Science of Safety." *Front Integr Neurosci.*, May 10, 2022; 16:871227. doi: 10.3389/fnint.2022.871227. PMID: 35645742; PMCID: PMC9131189.

8. Porges, S. W., "Polyvagal Theory: A Science of Safety." *Front Integr Neurosci.*, May 10, 2022; 16:871227. doi: 10.3389/fnint.2022.871227. PMID: 35645742; PMCID: PMC9131189.

How Joanne Established Inner Safety

Instead of engaging with the system, Joanne chose a different path. This time, she built her own self-regulation skills in a cutting-edge program offered by a recovered bulimic. The experiment was not only affordable, but it was also refundable if the process didn't produce results for Joanne. Good-ole capitalistic principles.

The program itself was inspired by two historical events. The first was United States Prohibition, a period when alcohol was banned nationwide. Despite the ban, alcohol consumption didn't completely cease; instead, it went underground, leading to the emergence of speakeasies and illegal distilleries. This underscored the fact that forced abstinence isn't an effective solution for addictive habits.

The bulimia program was also inspired by a 1970s "Rat Park" study, conducted by Canadian psychologist Bruce Alexander.[9] In the study, rats were placed in two different environments. One was a solitary cage with no social interaction or stimulation, while the other was a "Rat Park" filled with toys, tunnels, and other rats for social interaction. Both environments had access to two water bottles, one laced with morphine and the other just plain water.

In the solitary cage, the rats became heavily addicted to the morphine-laced water, consuming it over the plain water. However, in the "Rat Park," the rats largely ignored the morphine-laced water and preferred the plain water. The conclusion was that the solitary rats used the drug to cope with a lack of social interaction and stimulation, while the rats in the "Rat Park" did not need to use drugs.

The experiment Joanne signed up for promoted a voluntary 30-day abstinence from the binge-purge cycle. This allowed her to experience the benefits, addictive urges, and the actual (versus imagined) risks of living a life without bulimia. Unlike traditional counseling, a community was available for co-regulation and encouragement. Moreover, disclosing personal, private details was not a prerequisite for progress. The experience was more akin to going to a gym, a place filled with people striving to improve themselves, where the focus was on personal development, not food.

---

9. Alexander, B. K., Coombs, R. B., Hadaway, P. F. (1978). "The effect of housing and gender on morphine self-administration in rats." *Psychopharmacology*, 58(2), 175–179.

Phase 1

The initial 10 days involved extensive flexibility training, focused on building emotional flexibility. She became aware that her body was predicting danger even in safe circumstances, which explained why it had been so challenging to simply choose different thoughts. It was as though her body had post-traumatic stress disorder (PTSD) that had been operating outside her conscious awareness. The origin of the symptoms was less important than the awareness that her body was constantly predicting threats.

Virtual tools were provided based on the underlying principles of polyvagal theory, which explains how the autonomic nervous system regulates safety, connection, and threat responses through three hierarchical states: the ventral vagal state (social engagement and calm), the sympathetic state (fight-or-flight), and the dorsal vagal state (shutdown and dissociation). Crucially, this theory also highlights the flexibility of the nervous system and its capacity for neuroplasticity — the ability to rewire itself based on experience. The provided tools were akin to emotional treadmills that she could use repeatedly and privately on demand to help her release rigid thinking, adapt her identity to the role at hand, and build emotional flexibility. She began to understand that, like all other humans, there was a control panel to her nervous system, and there were knobs she could turn to transition from anxiety to safety whenever she wished.

Phase 2

The second 10 days, she developed the capacity for self-leadership. She worked to update her body, re-educating it to predict safety when her environment was indeed safe. She worked to intentionally build experiences of safety in her life during circumstances in which she noticed her body going into a fight-or-flight mode. These were small moments, like when she interacted with her husband, when she felt bloated, or when she was behind on a work deadline.

This effort required her to fall into the fear and threat in the moment, and offer herself compassion and soothing. She learned that a lot of deliberate planning was necessary to ensure her body consistently predicted safety. She began to deliberately schedule basics like sleep, water, nutrients, sunlight, movement, and connection. Simply winging it in this modern life didn't seem to work for her. She also worked to update her mind's predictions, completing daily assignments that explicitly devalued the benefits of being thin, and explicitly assigned a higher value to relationships and purposeful contribution.

Phase 3

The final 10 days, she developed her vision for the next year of her life and set an attention-commanding ambitious goal. To create consistent inner safety while pursuing this goal, she had no choice but to reconcile the mutually exclusive objectives to connect by winning approval for her physical appearance versus having the mental and physical bandwidth to be a present and nurturing mother, wife, and contributor. Because it was only for one year, she was willing to let her attention reorient to a non-food, non-body-related priority: the priority of pursuing her purpose in the world.

CREATING THE FUTURE

So far, Joanne is two years out with no signs of bulimia. Will she relapse? Perhaps. Relapse is one of the stages of change. However, Joanne now understands at a deep level that inner safety is a prerequisite to taking the lead in her own life. Like Joanne, we are all a small part of a very large system, and our unconscious behaviors and beliefs are all subject to influence from society, our inheritance, and our family of origin. And like Joanne, we have the most agency when we listen to what is true for our unique bodies — the vessel that carries us through life.

We are most able to pursue our purpose and lead others as parents and business executives after we establish self-leadership. Although it will always be uncomfortable to push the needle in our lives, we can arm ourselves with the capacity to create inner safety. As Abraham Lincoln famously said, "The best way to predict the future is to create it."

About Mark Carpenter

Mark Carpenter is a speaker, author, and facilitator on a mission to bring greater humanity into business. His speeches, workshops, and books focus on teaching "people skills" to create greater performance, connection, and engagement across teams and organizations, demonstrating how "soft skills deliver hard results."

For more information regarding our authors, please visit our webpage!
BestSellerPublishing.org/ExpertLeadership

CHAPTER 9

LEAD LIKE A PERSON

(THE IMPORTANCE OF
BEING MORE THAN A BOSS)

BY MARK CARPENTER

"We need more leaders who lead like people." I said it with conviction. This was such an obvious statement to me.

I was so confident in my point that I wasn't sure why I got a startled look from the person I was talking to when I said it.

Finally, she said, "But leaders are all people. If they aren't leading like people, what are they leading like?"

Hmmmm.

So, I shared this example.

I was working for a small software company, and by small, I mean 32 people. I managed marketing communications, including advertising and public relations. In this case, "managed" equals "I did it all." That's how small companies work.

I'd drafted a press release announcing the upcoming version of our flagship product. The release was reviewed by the product manager, my manager, and the chief technology officer. The final sign off would come from the CEO. We'll call him Mitch.

After Mitch reviewed the draft release, he called me into his office.

"This is good, but there's an important feature you left out." He went on to explain the feature and why it was essential. As I took notes, I wondered why no one else had brought it up. Based on the notes from

Mitch, I added a paragraph to the release about this feature, and Mitch approved it.

Just to be safe, I took the updated release to the CTO, Curt, for a second review. I wanted to make sure I had described the technology correctly from his perspective.

He read the paragraph and said, "Why did you add this? It's not in this version of the product. In fact, we're not 100% sure we can make it work, but we're hoping to have it ready for the next version."

I explained that Mitch had asked me to include it, and we decided it was a misunderstanding. Mitch must have thought it was in this version.

I went back to Mitch's office and explained, "I just talked with Curt. He said that feature is in the next version of the product, not this one. So, I'm going to have to drop that paragraph from the release."

Mitch responded, "I know, but leave it in there. Just write it in a way that's defensible."

Huh? I wasn't sure what that meant, so I asked.

The CEO said, "Just write it in a way that if anyone asks, we can tell them that we *meant* it was going to be in the next version. This feature will help us stand out from the competition."

I was confused and more than a little concerned.

"I'm not comfortable putting something in the release that we aren't sure we can develop," I said. "I think that could cause us problems."

At this point, Mitch stood up and pointed at me.

"Look," he barked, "you work for me. I sign your paycheck. You do what I tell you to do. Now get out."

At that moment, the conversation stopped being between two people. It was no longer Mitch talking to Mark. It was the CEO talking to a subordinate.

The conversation was between two positions.

When people lead like a position, they stop leading like a person. They lose sight of humanity and values for the sake of exercising hierarchy or protecting ego.

Let me make something exceptionally clear. Mitch was NOT a terrible human. Most of the time, he treated people well, was friendly, and had collaborative conversations. He had a family who loved him. He wasn't some ogre that had crawled out from under a rock and wormed his way into leadership.

But at certain moments, he slipped out of leading like a person and started leading like a position.

And he's not alone.

HOW DID WE GET HERE?

Few leaders wake up thinking, "I'm going to act like a tyrant today. I'm the boss, and I'm going to make sure everyone knows it."

How is it then that leaders show up more as a position than a person? We create the monsters we then must live with. Here's how.

When a front-line team needs a new leader, who typically gets selected to lead the team? In most organizations, the new leader is the best performer or the person with the longest tenure on the team. Sound familiar?

What training do most organizations give that new leader? The most common answer I hear is "none." But if they get any training at all, it's usually on topics like how to manage a budget, how to process payroll, how to create meeting agendas, and how to use certain processes or systems.

What kinds of skills does that develop in the new leader? Position skills.

A significant shift for first-time people leaders is the change from *doing work* to *leading people*. Yet few organizations focus the first-time leader's training on people skills. Then we're surprised when their teams are unhappy with their leadership.

I equate this to what happened with Victor Frankenstein in the Mary Shelley novel. Victor made a creature that he hoped would be a complete human. But when the creature turned out to be less than what Frankenstein expected, he didn't try to help the creature develop more human traits. He shunned the creature. He sent him away to live on his own in the wild. Then Frankenstein was surprised when the creature came back to destroy those he loved.

Have you seen that happen with new leaders? The organization gives them minimal leadership training at best, then senior leaders are surprised when the new leaders don't lead well.

Ancient Greek poet Archilochus said, "We do not rise to the level of our expectations. We fall to the level of our training." When we only train new leaders in position skills, is it any wonder they fall back on those skills when they face difficulties?

Just like Frankenstein, we create the monsters that we then must live with in our organizations.

Here's a real-life illustration. MJ led a team of five creative people at a software company. MJ felt like a good leader: the team was happy, they solved problems together, everyone was committed, and they got results. Most problems were more like speed bumps than hurdles. Life was good.

The small company was led by an energetic founder who encouraged an atmosphere of fun and growth. The company was making money and achieving most of its goals.

Then the economy dipped. Customers pulled back orders. Revenue goals were harder to hit. Tension increased. The angel investors took off their halos and ousted the founder CEO, bringing in a strict, by-the-numbers business leader to move the private company to an initial public offering or acquisition.

Suddenly, MJ found leadership more challenging. Budgets were cut. Staff was reduced. Pressure mounted on the remaining team members to get more results with fewer resources. MJ started making more demands of his team, closing the office door to get privacy, and avoiding difficult conversations.

MJ started leading like a position when his team most needed someone to lead like a person. As with most first-time people leaders, he had primarily been given position training, so when times got tough, he leaned on that training.

WHY DOES IT MATTER?

Lack of training for new leaders isn't a new phenomenon, so a natural question is, "Why should we care if someone leads like a position and not like a person?"

Let's start with a study from McKinsey & Company[10] that asked people, "Why did you leave your last job?" Take a look at the answers in the list below and in Figure A. Consider which of these can be influenced by the direct leader of the person leaving.

Top Reasons People Quit Their Jobs (% respondents):

1. Lack of career development and advancement (41%)

2. Inadequate total compensation (36%)

3. Uncaring and uninspiring leaders (34%)

4. Lack of meaningful work (31%)

5. Unsustainable work expectations (29%)

6. Lack of support for health and well-being (26%)

7. Unreliable, unsupportive people at work (26%)

8. Lack of workplace flexibility (26%)

Top Reasons People Quit Jobs
McKinsey & Company, 2022

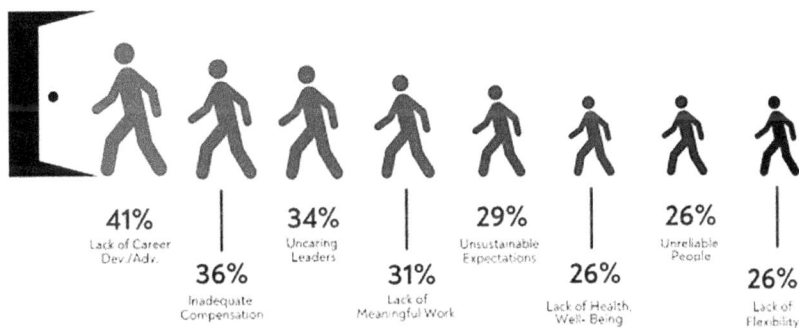

41%	34%	29%	26%
Lack of Career Dev./Adv.	Uncaring Leaders	Unsustainable Expectations	Unreliable People
36%	31%	26%	26%
Inadequate Compensation	Lack of Meaningful Work	Lack of Health, Well-Being	Lack of Flexibility

Figure A

How many of these problems could be reduced if the departing person's boss was leading more like a person than a position?

I suggest that most issues can be addressed by good people leaders, with the possible exceptions of geographic ties and travel demands.

---

10. For a brief on the study, look up the article "Why Employees Quit (And How to Keep Them)" by Wellable.

Maybe inadequate compensation is broader than the individual manager, but I think there are ways leaders can help overcome that issue, too.

A LinkedIn Learning study[11] supports the McKinsey findings, citing that 94% of employees say they would have stayed in a position longer if their company had invested in their career development. That's huge!

Managers who lead like a position are not concerned about employee development. They're concerned about their own standing and maintaining hierarchal power.

I think both studies show that poor people leadership has a direct impact on employee retention and its unpopular reflection: high turnover.

Additional research has highlighted the impact direct-line leaders have on morale, productivity, and engagement. Nothing much — just key factors in a company's output.

HOW TO LEAD LIKE A PERSON

Type "most important leadership skills" into a search engine and you'll get lists varying from six to twenty-six items long. Clearly that's too much to put on a new leader. But many of the "top" lists for leadership skills feature overlap among the skills listed. I propose three skills that will help new leaders lead more like people and bring benefits like improved productivity, lower turnover, and increased morale.

Listen intently: You've likely heard a lot of adverbs connecting to listening. Active listening. Focused listening. Empathetic listening. Critical listening. Appreciative listening. Listening intently encompasses all of those.

Intently is an adverb defined as "in a firmly or steadfastly fixed or directed way, as with the eyes, ears, or mind."[12] This isn't how we listen most of the time, and it's not critically important to listen intently much of the time. As a result, we don't focus much on learning the skill of listening intently.

---

11. The full LinkedIn Learning article is "The Rise and Responsibility of Talent Development in the New Labor Market."

12. From dictionary . com

Listening intently is a skill that helps new leaders support and build their teams. It requires practice and effort. And it pays huge dividends in understanding and solving problems. When leaders listen intently, team members feel valued and connected to the organization. When you lead like a person, you listen intently.

Communicate intentionally: We've been talking for years by the time we enter the workforce. As a result, communication can be taken for granted. We typically speak the same language as those we're leading, so communication should be easy.

Often, it is. But when challenging times arise, how we speak and how others hear what we say is more important. New leaders especially need to be intentional about how and what they communicate to their teams, their peers, and their leaders.

Communicating intentionally takes into consideration not only sharing what we need people to do but *why* they should do it. When leaders communicate intentionally, they build greater understanding and inspire action. They help people connect their personal values to company values. Communicating intentionally is not about communicating more but about how we communicate crucial information at crucial times.

Recognize individually: Few of the lists of leadership characteristics included recognizing people specifically. However, recognizing individually supports qualities such as character, generosity, positive attitude, relationships, servanthood, respect, trust, and positivity that appear on many lists of leadership traits.

Recognizing individually is not about throwing a party or tapping into corporate reward programs when someone does their job. It's about noticing when people are making an effort and showing them simple, day-to-day appreciation for their contributions.

Recognizing individually brings gratitude into the workplace. I've heard people say, "My employees get recognized twice a month. It's called a paycheck." A paycheck is *not* a form of recognition. A paycheck is fulfillment of a contract for work done. It's a base-level transaction.

Recognizing individually helps people feel a connection to their team and their company that powerfully enhances motivation and engagement. When people feel seen as individuals, they want to give more.

MY MISSION

I'm on a mission to create more first-time leaders who lead like people and not like positions. Why? Because I wish someone had helped me develop people-leadership skills earlier in my career.

Remember the story of MJ, the new manager who slipped into leading like a position when times got tough? I'm MJ. The story is mine.

I want to help companies build better first-time people leaders by providing the skills of listening intently, communicating intentionally, and recognizing individually.

I invite you to join me. Everyone will benefit from a world filled with leaders who lead more like people.

For more information regarding our authors,
please visit our webpage!
BestSellerPublishing.org/ExpertLeadership

About David R. Clark

David R. Clark is a man who has faced some of life's most daunting challenges and emerged with a deeper faith and a powerful message of hope. A former Alabama Assistant Attorney General, Judge Advocate General, and private attorney, David's life took an unexpected turn after sustaining debilitating injuries during his service in Iraq, leaving him 100% VA disabled. But instead of giving up, David chose to channel his experiences into something meaningful.

With resilience and determination, he pursued further education, earning a PhD in Interdisciplinary Studies from Amridge University and a Master's in History from Liberty University. His love for learning continues as he actively works toward a second PhD in History.

David's journey through hardship has profoundly shaped his writing. He has authored nine Amazon #1 best-selling books, each resonating with readers across multiple categories. He also co-authored a tenth book that achieved similar success.

For more information regarding our authors,
please visit our webpage!
BestSellerPublishing.org/ExpertLeadership

CHAPTER 10

STEWARD LEADERSHIP

(LEADING WITH PURPOSE
AND ACCOUNTABILITY)

BY DAVID CLARK

[Author's Note: The following is based on my doctoral dissertation, an adaptation of which I published in 2023 as Steward Leadership: Jesus' Leadership Model.]

Leadership is difficult to define. There is no consensus as to its definition. "There are almost as many different definitions of leadership as there are people who have tried to define it."[13] The modern study of leadership grew in the 20th century as scholars began researching the matter. With ever-increasing scholarship on leadership, the concept and definition of leadership has been, and continues to be, an evolving matter. The number of university programs and degrees dedicated to it has mushroomed over the last few decades. Peer-reviewed scholarly journals and professional journals centered on leadership have arisen and grown.

The reason for this exponential growth in the study of leadership, at least to some degree, is the fact that all are affected by it. With good leadership, everyone prospers. Conversely, with poor leadership, almost everyone suffers. In a world, much like the last couple of centuries, where people have more discretion in who the leader is, it is now more

---

13. Northouse, Peter Guy, *Leadership: Theory and Practice*, 8th ed. (Los Angeles: SAGE, 2019), 1.

important than ever to understand more abundantly what constitutes a good leader.

Even with the numerous definitions, there are some aspects of leadership for which there is growing agreement. There even seems to be an increasing consensus that leadership is mostly seen as a process where someone influences others to work toward a common goal. More specifically, leadership includes these four key aspects:

1. **Leadership is a process:** It's a back-and-forth, give-and-take interaction between the leader and the followers.

2. **Leadership involves non-coercive influence:** Leaders don't force people to follow; they inspire and guide them.

3. **Leadership brings meaningful change toward a common purpose:** Leaders work with their followers to achieve important goals.

4. **Leadership happens in a group:** Both the leader and the followers are active participants.

Looking at leadership this way, it's clear that it's not about having certain qualities or traits. Leaders aren't born with a special set of characteristics that make them good leaders. Instead, good leaders make conscious choices to prioritize certain things, which translates into good leadership.

WHAT IS A STEWARD?

A steward is someone who has been given the responsibility to care for someone else's resources/property. Steward leadership applies stewardship principles to leadership. The crux of the model is that the steward cares for the owner's resources in a proactive manner in order to achieve the owner's goals.

This means balancing the needs of different people in an organization, like shareholders, managers, employees, and the community. Key parts of steward leadership include making wise decisions about limited resources, showing self-control, considering the common good, and balancing faith and family, all with the foremost priority being to accomplish or exceed the owner's expectations and goals.

STEWARDSHIP AND ITS ROOTS

Stewards and their respective stewardships have been written about throughout history. The Old Testament, as one example, begins with stewardship principles when God gives Adam dominion over the Earth and a charge to care for the Garden of Eden. Other prime examples in the Old Testament are Abraham's steward, who was tasked with finding a wife for Isaac, Eliakim, who was steward to King Hezekiah, and, among others, Joseph, who was sold into Egypt.

From these Old Testament stewards, five distinct principles come to light.[14] Additionally, Kent R. Wilson observed a few stewardship themes from the Old Testament as well, as we'll see later.[15] These principles are that God owns everything, humans represent God on Earth, stewards are given authority, Joseph is a model steward, and there's a danger in the steward beginning to act as if he were the owner. Themes of stewardship in the Old Testament include acting on behalf of the owner, recognizing God's sovereignty, and the trust between the master and the steward.

In the New Testament, the perfect example of a steward is Jesus Christ, fully doing His Father's will. Additionally, Jesus taught several parables about stewards: the Parable of the Talents, the Parable of the Faithful and Wise Steward, the Parable of the Barren Fig Tree, and the Parable of the Unjust Steward. These parables teach important lessons like accountability, character, building relationships, aligning with the master's goals, and rewarding faithful stewards. Paul's letters emphasize that stewards must be faithful and are called by God, showing that all Christians are stewards of the gospel and of each other.

Steward leadership is about balancing resources and achieving goals while maintaining ethical and relational integrity. Steward leadership is the model that best reflects this balance.

---

14. Wilson, Kent R., *Steward Leadership*, 50.
15. Wilson, Kent R., *Steward Leadership*, 57.

THE RISE OF STEWARD LEADERSHIP TODAY

The English word "steward" has been around for a long time, first appearing in early English translations of the Bible. It originally meant "keeper of the hall" and referred to someone managing another person's household or property. Stewardship is different from trusteeship, as stewardship involves actively managing resources responsibly.

Steward leadership first appeared in the Western world during the American colonial era. Today, it is often linked to managing church finances, but stewardship principles apply more broadly than that.

Research into steward leadership began in the late 1980s to understand altruistic behavior in leaders who prioritize their organization's goals over personal gain. Agency theory, common in business, assumes agents (managers) act in their own interest, often conflicting with the owner's goals. To align interests, owners must provide incentives and consequences.

In contrast, steward theory assumes stewards act in the organization's best interest, putting the owner's goals first. Steward leaders promote personal growth, teamwork, and ethical management. Steward principles apply to various organizations, including businesses, nonprofits, schools, churches, and environmental groups. For steward leadership to succeed, stewards must be motivated by selflessness.

Even today, many believe that stewardship is an element of other leadership models, for example, servant leadership. Scholars in the 1990s began looking at stewardship not as an element, but as a leadership model in and of itself.

In 1989, J. Robert Clinton identified stewardship among four biblical leadership models: stewardship, harvest, shepherd, and servant. He regarded the stewardship model as the most foundational of the biblical models for all leaders, emphasizing accountability to God.

In 1993, David Birkenstock discussed Christian leadership at a seminar in South Africa, initially recognizing servant leadership but arguing that steward leadership better fits Christian leadership. He highlighted the stewards' roles in biblical times, emphasizing their trustworthiness, accountability, and reliability. Unlike servants, stewards managed their master's resources and were fully accountable to them, making stewardship a more comprehensive leadership model.

Also in 1993, Peter Block proposed using stewardship principles in corporate organizations, advocating for decentralized decision-making. He contrasted stewardship with traditional leadership, which centralizes power. Block emphasized service and long-term goals over self-interest, suggesting that stewardship supports broader community and ethical considerations.

In 2004, Peter Brinckerhoff applied steward leadership to nonprofit organizations, stressing that these entities belong to the community, not the operators. Operators must care for the organization as they would for someone else's property.

In 2016, Kent R. Wilson significantly structured the steward leadership model. He defined steward leadership as managing and growing organizational resources efficiently to achieve the owner's objectives. Wilson identified four key points about steward leadership:

1. Stewarding has two main goals: efficiency and growth

2. A steward both manages resources and leads (as in influences) people

3. Stewards do not own the resources they manage

4. The steward's main goal is to achieve the owner's plans and purposes

Wilson expanded stewardship beyond mere resource management to also include leading and influencing people, aligning closely with biblical stewardship practices. In reviewing both servant leadership and steward leadership, Wilson found that servant leadership is a subset of steward leadership. In my research, steward leadership is the next step that builds upon the principles laid out in servant leadership.

THE ELEMENTS OF STEWARD LEADERSHIP

In its most basic form, steward leadership consists of the relationship between the steward leader and the owner and the relationship between the steward leader and the followers.

The relationship the steward leader has with the organization's boss is essential in that it sets the parameters for how the steward leader should move forward with his or her stewardship of the organization. The following is a list I developed to flush this relationship out:

- The owner designates the leader. It is a calling issued by and through covenant.

- The owner prepares the leader in advance.

- The owner communicates objectives to the leader and to the people.

- The owner endows the leader with what is necessary to succeed.

- The owner has complete trust and confidence in the leader.

- The owner will support the leader in every way possible.

- The leader is faithful and obedient to the owner such that they will follow the owner's objectives no matter what.

The relationship between the leader and the followers can be described in the following terms:

- The leader sees an opportunity to lead as a calling, and not one that the leader takes upon themself.

- The leader communicates the mission to the people.

- The leader will be compassionate to the people.

- The leader makes things right for the followers of the organization.

- The leader is not only there to fix things for the followers in the organization, but for everyone everywhere.

- The leader will follow the owner no matter what, even if the followers initially reject the leader.

- Notwithstanding the followers' initial rejection, the leader does not get angry but perseveres in pursuing the owner's objectives in gentleness.

- The leader takes upon themself accountability for their and the followers' wrongs and failings.

- The followers improve because of the leader's unfailing compassion extended to them.

- The leader embodies the covenant relationship between owner and the followers. The leader does not own anything but rather is a representative of the owner to the people.

Based on the descriptions of the relationships the leader has with the owner as well as the relationship the leader has with the followers, the following is a list of the elements for steward leadership:

- Working with the understanding that all resources come from the owner, the steward leader, by and through covenant, prioritizes strict compliance to the owner, putting the owner first, and utilizing all resources afforded to the steward in accordance with the owner's will in order to bring all glory to the owner.

- Building and maintaining, through service among other measures, a relationship of trust with the organization's owner and with the followers.

- Putting the organization owner's objectives first, which includes altruistically putting the good of the organization above self.

- Always living beyond reproach and engaging in ethical/moral leadership and management.

- Influencing human followers by drawing out the best in each follower.

- Utilizing all talents, skills, and abilities in a manner that most effectively and efficiently accomplishes, or, if possible, exceeds, the owner's objectives.

- Providing accountability, given that the steward is not the owner, for how they steward resources and influence people.

- Ensuring and protecting the long-term success of the organization.

- Considering the effect the organization's actions may have on the environment in which the organization functions.

Steward leadership is one of the newest leadership models. Although the model has its contemporary roots beginning in the late 1980s and early 1990s, it lacked form and function. Those who identified it did not move beyond theory to develop any structure until the work of Kent R. Wilson. I have taken Wilson's research and moved steward leadership from a structure of traits and characteristics to a model that fits within the process of leadership. Now, research can move into the case study phase.

For more information regarding our authors,
please visit our webpage!
BestSellerPublishing.org/ExpertLeadership

About Jan Schaffner

Jan is a lover of God and a FREEDOM FIGHTER! She is a Mom and a Gramma to her amazing growing family. She is a published author of a FREEDOM Series and a Ministry Director; a Kingdom of God discipler, equipper and trainer. Her passion is to set captives free to fully embrace their truest identities and Kingdom destinies.

For more information regarding our authors,
please visit our webpage!
BestSellerPublishing.org/ExpertLeadership

CHAPTER 11

THE HEALED LEADER
(TRANSFORMING TRAUMA INTO POWER AND PURPOSE)

BY JAN SCHAFFNER

"Healed and Whole! Courageous and Bold! Wise and Powerful!" These were my "hopeful" annual goals for the start of each new year. After all, with a clear vision, it just requires determination, commitment, and great action plans, right?

The problem was that somehow, it wasn't working. Each year was proving my best strategies weren't getting the desired results. Losing 20 lbs. by Valentine's Day. No. Maybe by July 4th? Courageous, however, not able to confront those difficult people and situations? Bold, yet too concerned about what others thought of me? Somehow, my emotions were speaking louder than my best intentions.

After years of executive leadership, a change of heart was apparently needed. After 25 years of managing and leading people, I was exhausted. Ultimately, breakthroughs would be found at the deepest foundation of my core identity. They would be accessed by healing trauma buried deep in my emotions. They would be found in becoming "un-sabotaged" with a renewed mind.

Throughout my life, I've learned some freedom "keys" that are required to unlock many of those mind-traps, self-sabotaging lies, and limiting-belief boxes. After studying and researching healing modalities for years, it was time to find those hidden revelations still needed for myself.

My core message for over 15 years had been on freedom and whole-ness for spirit, soul, and body. However, retiring early, I found myself burned out. After resting for a whole year and seeing naturopaths, following all the health protocols, improvements were happening. Next, I enrolled in intensive inner healing processes. I learned much more about my brain and some of my faulty programming. Knowing that we're tri-part beings put me on a quest to be healed of all trauma that seemed to surface when it was least welcome. It was time to be fully healed.

My calling as a "freedom fighter" was becoming more evident. Age was still in my favor for pursuing my passion for helping others to be healed, whole and free. After several years of training, I was invited to help direct a Transformation Wholeness Center in our region. It turned into a seven-year adventure to help men and women of all ages receive healing in their spirits, souls, and bodies, with numerous physical healings documented. It was on-the-job training for much of what I'm sharing in this chapter. My own transformation was happening while I was helping others. It was one of the most rewarding times in my life.

BECOMING THE MESSAGE

With 2018 approaching, our team was asked to bring physical and emotional healing strategies to the front lines of our community. Our goal: facilitate trauma healing for homeless women during their transi-tion into the local shelter. We quickly found that what worked for the CEOs of companies worked for the women coming off the streets after being devastated by life.

Many had been trafficked. Most had been severely abused. Some had served time in prison. They were addicted or trying to get free from something. They had lost hope of having a normal life. They had been so traumatized that triggers were normal. Trust levels were low. After several sessions with our team, we documented a huge success rate. Women began to have hope. They received deep levels of healing that allowed many to see life through new lenses. Many went on to become completely transformed.

The year 2019 brought additional opportunities. While at a confer-ence on cultural mountains of influence, the economy, and media, mountains were highlighted to me. I also knew I was going to start writing about my core message on 3D Transformation. I'd had many years of classroom training, and now I had first-line, hands-on proof of hundreds of people being set free, healed and whole. My own healing was apparent to many people, who were amazed by my personal breakthroughs. I knew writing and capturing it all was my next step. I started writing the first volume in my Freedom series. It was a 30-Day Devotional. It was published that year and came out just as COVID became reality.

Stand Firm to be Free! was prophetic with regard to spiritual alignment as we all learned how to not be shaken with all the changes. Our shelter and centers were forced to close. I knew it was time to write the next two volumes on soul and body alignment. My core messages were now converging.

As 2020 progressed, I was learning how to write from my daily healing journals. At the same time, I was learning how to intermittent fast with results that seemed miraculous. After four months, I had lost 40 lbs. and healed five chronic conditions through fasting and autophagy. My high blood pressure numbers dropped to below normal. All long-term inflammation and pain vanished and my pre-diabetic counts went back to normal. Even my plantar fasciitis was healed. My next two volumes on soul and body healing were published to complete the trilogy.

My own life was becoming more wonderful. Sadly, at the same time, my husband was becoming very sick. He had been diagnosed with cancer years before, but it had been in remission for seven years. It had now come back with a vengeance. His bone scan showed Stage 4 terminal cancer. His prognosis was three months, which turned out to be correct. He passed peacefully into Heaven in January 2021.

It was a very challenging season for me, and thankfully the preceding several years of my life had prepared me. With my writing, ministry, and healing, my life was full of God's amazing grace. As 2022 came into view, it was time to start a new chapter. My team launched a Women's Hub called "Arise & Shine Freedom." I also started my personal ministry focused on setting captives free in 2023.

We're making a difference in our community as cultural catalysts and reformers. Our long-term vision is to have a Hope Transformation Center bring healing and wholeness to this Mid-Willamette Valley Region in Oregon. It's interesting to note that the Willamette River was named by the Indigenous peoples and means "death and dying." The white men had brought their diseases when settling the land in the 1800s. Our team is believing for our beautiful Willamette Valley to be a place of healing and restoration.

It's now been three years since my husband's passing. I've learned much during this season of change and transition. My soul has been set free, my mind has been renewed, and my body has been healed. My best years are ahead of me. The strategies my team and I have implemented are coming from years of brain science and testing on people of all ages and facets of life. Both men and women seem to benefit equally.

Our bodies are designed to heal naturally. Our brains are wired to become like a command central for our lives, much like a computer system. And just like computers, we must keep our hard-drives virus free. Over the years, I've seen people in every walk of life get rebooted and restored by applying these simple principles. Once viruses (wrong beliefs and lies) get deleted and trauma gets released, we have seen dramatic emotional and physical healings happen hundreds of times. Doctors will be the first to tell you that 80% or more of all diseases are related to stress and anxiety. We have found this to be true.

FREEDOM TO BE: BOLD, COURAGEOUS, HEALED, AND WHOLE

Let me explain what happens when a traumatic event occurs in your life at any time. First of all, your brain is capable of both recording and deleting events much like a recorder would. This is called neuroplasticity. When trauma occurs, your brain records it just as we experienced it at the age we were when it happened. If trauma happens to a three-year-old, it will be hot-wired in with the lies believed at the time. For example: the abuser says it was your fault. The trauma, pain, and lie are all imprinted and then stored in the reticular formation of your brain.

So, if someone is physically assaulted as a child, every negative, highly charged emotion is also recorded along with lies or beliefs attached to the trauma. If not healed, the trauma and the lie stay embedded and intact. (They remain until healed or removed intentionally.) With every similar event that accesses the memory, your brain will reinforce any lies with beliefs that were hot-wired into your memory. The fight-or-flight hormones with physiological responses are accessed when you have a flashback or a triggering moment. This explains what happens when a 50-year-old man has a temper tantrum like a 5-year-old child. He is reliving trauma triggered by a current event. The source event happened when the child was five. That memory is still actively causing him as a grown adult to feel powerless. It's time for healing and freedom.

The super good news is this: It's possible to delete those lies and get those memories healed. You actually have had PSTD from the trauma-based recorded memory. This is not a permanent condition as some would have you believe. Even with a lifetime of faulty beliefs, your brain can be healed, the lies deleted, and your mind transformed. Once the lie has been removed, your mind will be ready for your new truth. Ask for *truth* that should be the opposite of the trauma-based lie. Write it down. Your mind can now be renewed with that belief in an active transformation process. After removing the lie-based trauma beliefs, you'll feel freer. You're now ready for part two, which involves reprogramming, renewing, and rewiring your brain.

As an example, let's say you're in a leadership position and you're believing a lie that tells you you'll never measure up to the expectations of those around you. You know you're smart and capable, yet you keep getting sabotaged by limiting beliefs. Lies became embedded when as a child, you were severely punished for not performing jobs perfectly enough. You grew up believing you could never measure up. That was a lie-based belief supported throughout your life. Your brain worked hard to support that belief because you chose to agree with it. Your mind would search and look for data to support your "I'll never measure up" lie. It would find supporting evidence and constantly re-enforce the very thing you needed to be free of. To get free, it's an easy process, as stated above.

In the freedom-healing process, forgiveness is a huge key. It's important to release those who helped you believe lies throughout your lifetime. It's also important to break agreements with faulty beliefs, completely deleting them all from your thinking. In reality, your brain will support whatever you agree with. Once the lies are gone, the truth will be easy to access. Once you have your truth, your mind can be transformed and healed by building new brain pathways. It will start as a little dirt trail and become a super highway. Rewire your brain by speaking, decreeing, and blessing your spirit, soul, and body with truth for up to 63 days. It takes that long to renew your mind, especially when you've lived with sabotaging beliefs for years.

Renowned brain scientist Carolyn Leaf will tell you there are no shortcuts to mind renewal. Romans 12:2 (NIV) is a good verse to study as you're becoming set free from the past: "Be transformed by the renewing of your mind." The Truth will set you free!

Does this process sound too good to be true? I challenge anyone reading this to give it a try. Follow this process or perhaps make an appointment to have a trusted person help you to get free and healed. Many are waiting for authentic, truly healed leaders to emerge. The battles we face are always related to our true identity and ultimate destiny calling. Let me leave you with this thought: God often uses our deepest pain as the launching pad of our greatest purpose and calling!

For more information regarding our authors,
please visit our webpage!
BestSellerPublishing.org/ExpertLeadership

ABOUT DENNIS DUFF, MSU &
ELLEN EATOUGH, MA

Ellen Eatough, with a Master's Degree in East-West Psychology, has been an intimacy coach and sexual healer since 1991 and has conducted numerous in-person workshops on sexual-spiritual fulfillment and intimate communication nationwide.

Dennis Duff, a successful spiritually centered business owner, trainer, and counselor/coach to couples with relationship difficulties, spent over 40 years in the "inner circle" studying with a fully enlightened spiritual teacher and tantric master.

Together Dennis and Ellen run Ecstatic Life, LLC, with the mission to uplift humanity by transforming intimate relationships. They provide breakthrough programs that help older singles and couples experience the greatest love of their lives.

For more information regarding our authors,
please visit our webpage!
BestSellerPublishing.org/ExpertLeadership

Chapter 12

The R.E.A.L. Formula™ for Epic Love

(Leadership in Marriage and Long-Term Relationships)

by Dennis Duff, MSU & Ellen Eatough, MA

Are you leading your love life — or is it leading you?

Many people don't realize this but, whether you're single and looking for love or in a long-term relationship, an invisible yet powerful force shapes your experience of love and intimacy. It's like computer software running in the background that totally dictates our love life — for better or worse. This includes what we feel we deserve in love, how we interact with our mate or a prospective partner, our emotional availability for love and connection, and so much more.

We call this force your **Relationship Reality Field**™.

The good news? You have the power to take leadership in your love life and align this field with your deepest desires. Through decades of coaching singles and couples, we've developed a proven framework — **The R.E.A.L. Formula for Epic Love** — to help you become the leader of your love life.

But first, let us share how this journey unfolded for us.

DENNIS'S STORY: RISING FROM THE ASHES

I'm standing in the ashes of my northern California dream home. Smoke curls from the remains of 35 years of memories. My neighbor's frantic call had interrupted our Lake Tahoe vacation: "Dennis, a wildfire is racing through our neighborhood!" Now, surveying the destruction, I have no idea this is just the beginning.

Six months later, my wife leaves me. Within a year, we're divorced. The life I'd built, my marriage to a former Miss California, and my wine country home on five acres — gone. Now my whole life is ashes.

But I've spent four decades practicing spiritual discipline with an enlightened master, and I know there's a deeper lesson here. I look inward, asking myself, *How did I contribute to the demise of our marriage? What are the lessons to be learned here?*

Eventually, as I sift through the emotional debris, a spark ignites inside me: a burning desire to create the deepest, most loving relationship imaginable. But there's one problem — I haven't dated in 50 years. Despite my fear, I dive in.

I sign up for every dating site I can find. After 10 dates, I'm getting my feet wet. After 20, I know what I want: emotional depth, humor, intelligence, and vulnerability. By date 30, I'm frustrated. *Where the heck is she?*

In desperation, I reach out to a psychic friend. She tells me, "Don't worry. She's out there. Write her a letter describing how it *feels* to be with her." So, I do. I pour my heart into that letter, describing in detail the joy, passion, and intimacy I long to create in this relationship with her. Holding this vision, I continue my quest for love.

Meanwhile …

ELLEN'S STORY: THE KEY TO FINDING "THE ONE"

I have high standards: I want the ultimate sexual/spiritual relationship! I'm an intimacy coach and sexual healer, and raised two sons during a 20-year marriage. In my 60s, I'm thinking, *If I want to find my last great love and life partner, I better get busy!*

Naturally, I want chemistry, but after going on a lot of first dates, I'm getting nowhere. So, I get intentional. Even if there's no initial chemistry, I give promising men four dates to see if attraction can grow. Twelve high-quality men later, I'm still searching for "The One."

Determined, I go to an Ayahuasca healing ceremony. The medicine tells me, *The key is vulnerability — but you have to go first.* I resist. *What?! I don't want to be vulnerable first! Let him go first, then I'll be vulnerable.*

Soon after, Dennis finds me online, and we meet at an Italian restaurant. Studying him across the table, I think, *He's not my type. Handsome, yes. Interesting, for sure. But romantic attraction? No.*

Yet something's clearly going on. Our waiter, Patricio, is fluttering around us like Cupid himself, bringing us free wine tastings and tiramisu.

Within three months, I'm totally in love with this man. Dennis is everything I've wanted … and so much more! And he tells me, "Your vulnerability was what initially attracted me."

What Is Happening?

When more raging California forest fires bring in toxic smoke, we rent a little RV and head to the coast for some clean air and outdoor recreation. But the thick smoke follows us, and we're stuck inside this tiny RV for four days. On the second day, we're discussing how we want to create our life together.

Suddenly, Dennis's deceased spiritual master appears to me in a vision. He says, "You have to be open to all possibilities, including possibilities beyond anything you've imagined. You have to think much bigger!" What does this mean?

After we're living together, we're lying in bed feeling very grateful for our life. Boom! I get another download from the universe: "This relationship is not just for you. You need to share this with the world!" Well … Okay!

This led us to develop The R.E.A.L. Formula for Epic Love. It's a framework rooted in ancient wisdom, quantum physics, and modern neuroscience. It's helped us, our clients, and countless others take leadership in their love lives. And here it is:

The R.E.A.L. Formula™ for Epic Love

R = Recreate your Relationship Reality Field™

E = Elevate your frequency

A = Avoid assumption traps

L = Live and love generously

Let's explore how these principles can transform your love life.

R = RECREATE YOUR RELATIONSHIP REALITY FIELD™

What's a Relationship Reality Field?

Your **Relationship Reality Field** is your fundamental perspective and way of being with regard to your love life. It's shaped by your childhood imprinting, personal relationship experience, and influence from friends, family, and the media. It's based on the past and is typically unconscious.

Yet it's very powerful because it determines the quality of your love life. Once you recognize this, whether you're single or in a long-term relationship, you're in a position to radically transform this reality field to align with the love life you want.

How to Recreate Your Relationship Reality Field:

- Don't let yourself be blinded by superficial desires. Instead, uncover the essence of what will make you truly happy in a relationship, beyond the list of what you think you want ... to clarify your new intentions.

- Infuse your clear new intentions with the emotions you long to experience as a result of its fulfillment. These might be emotions like deep love, joy, gratitude, playfulness, or passion. This will shift your electromagnetic field to draw your desired outcome to you. If resistance shows up, unearth unconscious core beliefs that thwart your ability to attract a high-quality partner, or get out of a rut in your current relationship, and release them once and for all.

When you've done that, you'll begin to notice positive, often unexpected, shifts in your relationship experience, and you're on a new trajectory toward creating the love life you desire — like the people whose stories we briefly relay below.

Hugh and Beth's Story:

Hugh and Beth, married 32 years, come to our couples' retreat feeling like "terrible role models" for their grown children because of constant fighting. Hugh admits he's pressured Beth for decades to wear extremely sexually provocative clothing in public to fuel his arousal, leaving her feeling objectified and defensive, like a ticking time bomb.

During the retreat, Hugh realizes his demands stem from a misguided attempt to feel closer to Beth. Committing to change, he works with her to create more loving and authentic ways to connect. Together, they shift their Reality Fields and leave the retreat with a renewed sense of intimacy.

On a follow-up call, they share that even their children have noticed the dramatic reduction in their fights. Hugh and Beth say their breakthrough was life-changing — and worth the ongoing effort.

Rachel's Story:

Rachel, a 62-year-old psychologist, was certain she wanted a partner who earned more than she did. But after deeper reflection, she realized her fundamental need was for security and financial stability.

With this clarity, she met Alan, a highly skilled bodyworker who earned less but excelled at managing money and making profitable investments. They married a few years later, and Rachel happily says, "I made Alan the CEO of our marriage," recognizing his strengths complemented hers perfectly.

Clay's Story:

Clay's 27-year marriage ended in divorce, leaving him feeling like a failure and stuck in a rut of inadequacy. Unsure of what he wanted in a partner or if he was even capable of a fulfilling relationship, he decided to take leadership in his love life.

Through inner work, Clay released the negative patterns shaped by his parents' poor relationship modeling and began to envision a new kind of partnership. This shift in his Reality Field allowed him to attract Lisa, the greatest love of his life — a relationship he once thought was out of reach.

Each of the remaining components of The R.E.A.L. Formula further contribute to the overall goal of Recreating Your Relationship Reality Field.

E = ELEVATE YOUR FREQUENCY: HOW IT TRANSFORMS RELATIONSHIPS

Your emotional energy attracts similar energetic frequencies. When you elevate your frequency, you naturally resonate with and attract partners or experiences that match your higher vibration.

Modern theories indicate that we're all energy, and our frequencies subtly broadcast our internal state, attracting people of a similar vibration. The first time you fell in love, you were likely operating at an elevated frequency of joy, appreciation, and possibility. Over time, many couples drift into lower frequencies of routine, indifference, or criticism. Moreover, many singles looking for love get frustrated or negative about the types of relationship prospects they meet.

When you elevate your frequency, you attract and sustain higher-quality connections. You can lead yourself into a better love life by consciously uplifting your energy to attract high-value partner prospects or lead your current relationship back to a more joyful and loving life together.

> **David's Story:**
>
> David comes to us frustrated after his divorce, claiming all the women he meets are "too negative." But he soon uncovers a profound truth: he's attracting the skepticism and judgment he's putting out.
>
> We teach David about energetic resonance. By cultivating acceptance and joy — not as a tactic, but as a way of being — everything shifts. Within weeks, he reports meeting women who reflect his newfound optimism and zest for life.

> **Diane and Mark's Story:**
>
> Married 24 years, Diane is fed up with constant mutual fault-finding and tension. We encourage her to stop trying to change Mark and focus on elevating her own frequency. She begins appreciating small moments, expressing gratitude for Mark's efforts and approaching him with curiosity.
>
> Almost immediately, she feels better. Within a month, Mark naturally matches her higher frequency energy, transforming their home from tense to peaceful and tender.

A = AVOID ASSUMPTION TRAPS: THE SILENT SABOTEURS OF LOVE

Assumptions undermine intimacy. They often go unnoticed but shape how we perceive and interact with our mates or prospective partners.

Often, we believe something is absolutely true — when it's merely an assumption. The challenge is our assumptions are typically unconscious. This makes it almost impossible to recognize assumptions on your own. But when you get help recognizing and disarming your assumptions, it exponentially increases your ability to rapidly transform your love life.

If you get caught in Assumption Traps, it will hurt you. Your limiting assumptions will minimize your chances of finding a partner who will adore you and enthusiastically commit to building a life together. And over time, assumptions will keep you stuck in patterns that make your intimate relationship less than joyful.

> ### *Dennis and Ellen's Story:*
>
> Our personal story illustrates this principle. We both initially assumed we needed younger partners to match our energy and vitality, so we almost missed finding each other. How wrong we were! We quickly realized vital energy isn't about age but about lifestyle, spirit, and mindset.

> ### *Robert and Lisa's Story:*
>
> Robert and Lisa were trapped by assumptions about how love "should" be shown. Lisa believed Robert's quiet nature meant he didn't care, while Robert thought Lisa's need for words meant his actions weren't enough.
>
> When they recognize these are just assumptions — not facts — everything changes. With some guidance, they uncover each other's unique ways of expressing love and create new, meaningful ways to connect that honor them both.

L = Live and Love Generously: The Power of the Platinum Rule

And finally, the last part of the formula is to Live and Love Generously and Embody the "Platinum Rule," which goes beyond the well-known "Golden Rule."

The Golden Rule states: "Treat others how **you** would like to be treated," but the Platinum Rule advises: "Treat others how **they** would like to be treated." Moreover, the Golden Rule assumes others would want things the way you want them. The Golden Rule is ME-centered, whereas the Platinum Rule is centered on the other person. This is the key to loving generously.

> ### *Carla's Story:*
>
> Carla came to us wanting a list of first-date questions. Instead, we coached her to drop the "interview" approach and focus on creating a fun, relaxed experience for her dates.

As she shifted her focus, her dates became more at ease, revealing their best qualities. Carla found herself relaxing too, which helped her tune into how she felt with each person — making it easier to decide who was truly worth getting to know.

Anna and Tom's Story:

After 15 years of marriage, Anna and Tom are drifting apart — until they embrace the Platinum Rule. Tom starts asking Anna about her dreams, not just her day. Anna begins creating adventure dates, knowing Tom craves new experiences.

Their renewed generosity of spirit reignites their passion and deepens their connection in ways they never imagined.

TAKE LEADERSHIP OF YOUR LOVE LIFE

True leadership begins within. By applying The R.E.A.L. Formula, you can lead your love life with clarity, intention, and heart.

Unlike surface-level advice, this formula tackles the root of your relationship challenges. Transforming your inner world allows you to naturally attract and sustain the epic love you desire — whether you're seeking a partner or deepening an existing relationship.

Epic love isn't just for the young or the lucky. It's available to anyone willing to recreate their Relationship Reality Field, elevate their energetic frequency, overcome limiting assumptions, and live and love generously.

This process is simple, but not always easy. Transformation takes courage — and support can make all the difference. At Golden Love Academy, we guide individuals and couples through The R.E.A.L. Formula to create extraordinary, joyful, and deeply fulfilling love lives.

Yes, skills like writing a great online profile, the art of successful dating, improving communication, and enhancing your sex life are important — which is why we teach them. But without the internal transformation this formula provides, even the best "how-to" advice falls short.

Without The R.E.A.L. Formula, nothing works. With The R.E.A.L. Formula, everything works.

BEGIN YOUR JOURNEY TO EPIC LOVE

Epic love begins with two things: the courage to believe in love again and the wisdom to approach it with intention. Wherever you are on your path, The R.E.A.L. Formula meets you right where you are to help you create the love life you've always longed for. If you're ready, we're here to guide you.

Start your journey today with our **FREE training video and worksheet: "Your Epic Love Map"** at www.DennisandEllen.com. This is your first step to Recreating Your Relationship Reality Field.

"Your Epic Love Map" helps you uncover what will truly make you happy in a relationship — beyond the checklist of what you think you want. It reveals the deeper desires of your heart and clarifies your highest intentions for love so you can start manifesting them right away.

Visit www.DennisandEllen.com and take the first step toward creating the epic love life you deserve.

For more information regarding our authors,
please visit our webpage!
BestSellerPublishing.org/ExpertLeadership

About Andrew A. Wittig

Andrew Wittig, a seasoned entrepreneur and automotive business owner, balances his professional life with a deep commitment to his faith, mentoring others, and raising six children. His upcoming book explores how to have great spiritual conversations.

Andrew Wittig is an entrepreneur by nature who has owned several businesses. Presently, he runs a successful automotive collision repair facility. He is a very devout member in his faith community, and is involved in mentoring others in sharing their religious convictions. He and his wife are the proud parents of six gifted children, and enjoy quality family time. Wittig has another book being released early 2025, which shares ideas on ways to organically create conversations of a spiritual nature.

For more information regarding our authors,
please visit our webpage!
BestSellerPublishing.org/ExpertLeadership

CHAPTER 13

TAKING THE REINS

(THE POWER OF LEADING FROM THE FRONT)

BY ANDREW A. WITTIG

When I was a kid, I wanted to be just like my dad. He was always showing me how to do things. He owned his own landscaping and construction businesses, and he led people in our church; he was my superhero. I designed my life around what he thought was a great career path for me. I trusted his judgment because he always led me safely onto successful paths. He taught me what it meant to serve in my community on weekends, helping widows and cleaning up the streets of Las Vegas by painting over graffiti. I could talk to him about anything as a parent, and he got me through some of my toughest times emotionally as a young man.

When I was earning my Eagle Scout badge in the Boy Scouts of America at age 14, he was there to support me with whatever project I chose. When I was on varsity volleyball and going for the championship, he was cheering me on like he had taught me in every other sport my whole life. When I was preparing to serve as a full-time missionary for my church for two years (just like he had), he talked me through it all.

My dad showed me how to lead from the front my entire childhood. I was eager as a young adult attending college to do even better at life than he had. I was eager to lead in bigger ways than my dad had. It did not happen overnight. I switched careers, moved states, struggled, and overcame financial hardships and mental blocks, all while raising a young family and serving in my church and never once letting go of my faith. And through everything, I refused to let go of my quest to figure out how to lead. I felt like the secrets to great leadership were eluding me, no matter how many books I read or how many pep talks I got from my dad. It's been said that some lessons in life are caught ... not taught. Take swimming: you can spend all day in books learning about swimming, but until you get in the water and try, it's all just theory. That is how it is with leadership. Until you're out there working with and around people, it's hard to truly grasp the depth of what it takes to be a good leader.

One of my past ecclesiastical assignments involved me being in charge of the local missionary work of the congregation I attended. One of the responsibilities consisted of attending a quarterly meeting with counterparts from the other eight or nine congregations in the area in order to receive instruction from a regional leader over missionary work. As the meetings went on over the year, I noticed really fast that my counterparts were all "dead" and unenthusiastic about sharing the gospel. No wonder their congregations had no new convert results to show. The ones responsible for encouraging and motivating the members to invite others to learn more weren't even doing it themselves.

I committed to myself right then and there that I would be different, that I would lead from the front. Soon after, as I built up the courage to have more spiritual conversations with others, I began to see success. The success of having friends of mine come to church with me began to inspire other members to do the same, and we had an exceptional number of new converts that year. This greatly inspired the work that I'm doing today.

MOMENTUM FROM THE FRONT LINE

As you "take the reins" and begin leading from the front, others will soon follow, and your team will build momentum. It's not easy to notice when you're in a rut. Over five years into a new career field, I found myself in a deep rut. I felt like I was very unorganized and just all over the place. Sometimes, it just takes getting away, out to a seminar or retreat, to help you see your situation with new eyes. With these new eyes, I realized that leading from the front can even have an effect on something as simple as being organized at home.

As I got back from a training seminar and walked into my house I realized that I was such a slob. And my kids … I'm raising little slobs! This had to change. Yelling at my kids to clean their rooms never seemed to work, so I decided to start with me. How would my kids ever learn to accomplish their goals and dreams if dear old dad couldn't even keep his side of his bedroom clean? I had to start small. I began by clearing off my nightstand. I even polished it. It felt good.

The following day, I decluttered the floor next to my side of the bed and vacuumed. Now I wouldn't have to trip or stub my toes if I needed to get up in the middle of the night.

The next day, I completely cleaned our two-sink master bath counter and mirror. I even decided to keep a folded rag in the corner of the counter to wipe water droplets off the faucet, mirror, and counter after each time I used it.

By this time, my kids were starting to think that Dad was up to something. "Is he okay?" they asked my wife.

As I approached day four, I was feeling brave enough to tackle the organized chaos I called my desk. "Stay focused, and start small," I had to keep reminding myself. It's amazing what a few newly labeled file folders can do to create places for your "chaos" to go. Two hours later — desk cleaned and polished!

This whole time, as I was trying to get myself organizationally together, my kids had been silently observing. After about another two or three days, what did I begin to notice? Their beds were consistently being made, their floors were being cleaned and vacuumed, and their desks were being cleared off and made functional again. A miracle, some might say. But I would suggest otherwise. Especially as parents, our personal examples speak louder than our words. No one wants to follow a hypocrite, and neither do our children. In our own homes, as we lead from the front, the effects have the potential to change and influence generations.

THE CHALLENGE OF HYPOCRISY

I think that just about everyone has had an assigned leader or teacher who was uninspiring, unmotivating, and outright annoying to receive marching orders from. I'm sure it's because deep down, we felt that they were being hypocritical because their choice of leadership style was "do as I say, not as I do." The greatest sales teams, and even sports teams, are typically led by "grab-the-bull-by-the-horns" kind of people. Their vision, enthusiasm, and personal drive generally becomes contagious, and the other team members follow. If you want to have a winning sales team, coachable employees, or a successful sports team, then you're going to need to be the light that everyone follows through the darkness of self-doubt and defeat.

It's easy as the head of a sales team or organization to look down over the group and think, "Why are their numbers so low? Why can't they hit their quotas? When are they ever going to get with it? How will I ever reach my promotion goals with their poor performance?"

I found myself in that exact spot some years into my career in the financial industry. As a director of marketing, I couldn't seem to get anyone to produce in order to help me reach my personal promotion goals. It felt like I was having to drag them along, almost begging them to do their part. It wasn't until I was in a leadership seminar where it hit me: *No wonder my sales team wasn't producing anything. Their leader (me) wasn't doing anything. Why would they need to perform, if their fearless leader didn't have to?* This was a turning point in my career.

As I began to make my daily minimum calls and contacts, I began to generate sales, referrals, more sales, and ultimately, momentum. I also noticed that my team naturally became more coachable, and I didn't have to work nearly as hard to get them to do anything. As my personal activity and results soared, the team followed suit. Over that 90-day stretch, not only was I promoted to a position as a senior marketing director, but I also produced over $80,000 in personal commissions.

As human beings, I think we naturally want to follow doers — those worth emulating. Their passion, energy, and enthusiasm makes us want to be like them. As you lead from the front, your people will follow you because they respect you, not just because they have to.

THE VALUE OF INTROSPECTION

I'm in the process of teaching religious leaders how important it is to lead from the front when it comes to sharing the gospel with others. If they, as teachers, are struggling to find the words for what to say to invite others to come and see, how in the world are those that they lead ever going to feel capable of doing so? As I have heard, a general principle in leadership is that "your people will always do less than you do." If you're not producing adequate numbers, then neither will they. Monkey see, monkey do. One of the things I'm doing to provide a resource for these leaders is to publish a book that literally includes some of the daily casual conversations of a spiritual nature I have recorded in diary fashion over the last six years. I completely transformed from hating to hear about the subject of sharing to feeling totally "off" if I didn't naturally have a spiritual conversation with someone daily.

Leading a religious group, or any other organization for that matter, requires taking a hard look in the mirror to personally assess whether you feel capable enough to produce your desired result, your people have enough training to successfully produce a result, and you are willing to charge ahead and lead from the front. Take time to do some serious introspection. Are you setting an example on pace, production, and achievement? These can be hard questions to confront. It's challenging even considering communicating these introspective findings with the people who matter.

If you have any hesitation or self-doubt about your own capability, I guarantee your people are feeling even more inadequate. If necessary, take time to "sharpen the saw," as someone wise once said. Once you feel your proverbial "saw" is sharpened, make sure you help sharpen your people's "saw." Then, personally "pound the pavement" and show them the way to the "promised land."

CARRYING THE FIRE

To this day, as the oldest of six siblings, I still maintain a strong relationship with my dad. So far, with that lifelong proximity to my father, I'm the only entrepreneur as well. We talk almost daily about our life challenges, achievements, and new directions our lives are taking. He sees me as taking his leadership and role to the next level, which, of course, makes him proud.

As it turns out, my focus on missionary work was completely sparked by his enthusiasm for the joy he received from someone having a natural, spiritual conversation with him back in his 20s. His "spark" ignited a "flame" within me and helped me realize a talent I may never have discovered without the life he provided and the aspirations he instilled by example.

My youthful hunger for wisdom and knowledge, fueled by his encouragement, has now led to an enjoyable role reversal. Today, I now share with him, and the sounding board aspect of our relationship has become mutual. It's great to be able to be there and be the pillar of encouragement as my dad takes on a new phase in his life.

As parents, my wife and I have a natural hope that our children will build on the foundation we provided them and exceed our successes and joys. That rings true with leadership as well. The greater example of a leader we can provide today, whether in our homes or in our communities, the greater leadership you'll witness in the world tomorrow.

For more information regarding our authors,
please visit our webpage!
BestSellerPublishing.org/ExpertLeadership

About J.R. Vincent

J.R. Vincent is a force of creative energy. She's an artist who balances business, writing, and production design with the joyful chaos of raising six children. Her journey is a testament to the power of embracing new experiences and finding inspiration in the everyday. Vincent's commitment to community and faith underscores her belief in the power of connection and the importance of giving back. Look for her newest book, *Your Mom Never Said: Empowering Lessons Everyone Needs for a Happy Successful Life*, releasing soon.

For more information regarding our authors, please visit our webpage!
BestSellerPublishing.org/ExpertLeadership

CHAPTER 14

THE OBSERVATIONAL LEADER

(LEAD WHERE YOU STAND)

BY J.R. VINCENT

Fear was one thing I didn't learn until I was no longer a child. I was never afraid to be the first to ask or answer a question in school, or be at the head of the line. I shot my hand up whenever a volunteer was asked to pray or speak in church. I was always ready to cook even when it made my mom nervous because I was so young. I was happy to read the books I knew to anyone who would listen, especially my younger brothers. I loved being a part of big group performances in Girl Scouts.

For me, leading is just what you do when you want to make something happen. I was not afraid to stand out, or help, or look a little silly. I've been tall, friendly, and cheerful my whole life. I like to see people smile. I love it when people come together to do great things. Looking back, I can see how I became a leader one opportunity at a time by leading where I stand. Some people are born leaders. Some people are made leaders. But no matter where you are, you can lead where you stand.

My mom called me "big eyes" because I was always watching people, and "radar ears" when I would listen in on grown-up conversations. I longed to be like the adults I knew who were capable and talented. People listened to them. People followed them. I was always making plans and dreaming up projects. I was easily frustrated as a kid when I was told "no" because I was "too young." My mom said I had "big feelings." I call this same trait "passion" in my children. When you are six, no one expects you to get up in front of 200 people and recite a long poem, but I did. When you are seven, you aren't expected to know how to use a glue gun proficiently, but I could because I practiced late at night after everyone was in bed. I had drive and vision even then.

When I was asked to serve as president of our youth class at church at age 13, I said yes despite feeling inadequate. When I had the chance to learn how to use power tools and enamel paint, and then direct 100 other teenagers to do the same at age 17 — I did it. I was resented at times for being the teacher's pet, but I let it go. I wasn't the smartest in my graduating class, but I have always loved to learn. I've never shied away from helping someone in need, and I'm not afraid to work hard.

You don't have to be elected, hired, or assigned to lead. Leadership takes self-assurance and fearlessness. It takes love and understanding of people. It takes patience and perseverance and concern. You must sometimes sacrifice what you want to do now, for the greater goal you have in mind.

The Importance of Opportunity (In Its Many Forms)

Some people really are born leaders, but most are made. Leadership can be nurtured through education, training, and mentorship. We aren't all born with the same opportunities in life and that's okay. You have to start somewhere. Education is meant to help you learn what you don't know. My parents are not much for leadership. My mom would rather be under a rock hiding from answering to people, and my dad would rather be skipping it across water having some fun. So what can you do?

You can't blame where you came from for any of your problems; you have the internet. You have school and courses and libraries and a whole world out there that isn't going to wait for you. Find out what you don't know. I share a lot of this in my book, *Your Mom Never Said*. Because the truth is that a lot of us don't grow up hearing about principles of leadership and success. It's never too late to start leading where you live now. Sign up to serve in your community and attend local events. Participate in your local government and join groups that interest you.

At some point, once you've tried a lot of things and you've met a lot of people, you will start to feel like you've found "it." "It" is your community. "It" is the groups of people that make up your wider circles. What used to make the Daisy Girl Scouts think I was weird, I now get paid for. You'll find your groove, your "thing." Most of all, you'll start to notice that people rely on you as you take on more responsibility and show up for some of the hard things not everyone can or will do. That is leadership. You can have as much influence as you decide to.

Leaders see opportunities where others see challenges. Leaders feel pulled and prompted to make things happen, and they take action. Being a leader requires effort, change, and growth. You live somewhere where there are new things you haven't learned or tried yet. Put yourself out there and do something new. There are chances to serve and learn all around you. Things like cleaning up highways and sprucing up parks, delivering meals, and attending local arts events will bring you into close contact with new people and wider circles of influence. I have appreciated every chance I've had to meet and befriend older generations of people. They have their priorities straight and are always willing to pass on lessons they've learned. Best of all, they are endlessly encouraging of new and willing leaders, especially in today's world. So get out there.

Never be afraid to stand up for what you believe in at all times. I have made countless friends from sticking to what I know to be right and true. Like minds find each other. Serving where you stand starts when you put your two feet on the ground every single morning at home. Growing up, I tried to be a mentor to my youngest brother as much as I could. I tried to be there for him in the ways our parents did not know how to be. They really did their best, and they were much better parents than their parents. They're the first to admit they lacked skills. But we knew they loved us.

LOVE IS LEADERSHIP

I always pictured myself with a big family of my own someday. I expected that life would be good if I could keep helping those around me see how much better things can always be. Never apologize for high expectations.

Eventually, I found a man who was just as crazy as I was to marry. Our family is complete with six children. As if running businesses and leading in our church and community weren't enough, we're raising six capable, talented, strong-willed kids in 2025. I expect a lot of my little dragons. I would not call one of them "easy," but they are all incredible people who I have the privilege to lead into adulthood.

To lead is to learn to love. It's the answer to a call no one else can hear. It starts small. Leadership is caring more about others than you do about yourself for periods of time. As a mother, I can't go one day without someone "needing" me. My kids will walk right past their dad and come straight to me. He's a great dad, but he isn't "Master of the House" (feel free to hum that here). He calls me "Your Ladyship." I earned that title one day at a time. I was there every day of their lives. I fed them. I clothed them. I hauled home furniture to make each of our houses homes.

I teach everyone how to do everything: get dressed, brush teeth, tie shoes, cook, read, and do math. I budget. I plan every vacation. When something needs fixing, I fix it. When someone is hurt, I heal it. I am a nurse, counselor, chef, and teacher. I am the master and commander of our ship. "Is it 'mom clean'?" They must ask each other. My standards are high, but we have fun and we learn together. When I call, they better come running. They come running because they trust me.

The most exciting thing about who we call family is watching them grow and win. I see that my children are farther ahead as the amazing people they are because of where I came from. I learned and grew and taught them everything I know. Now they are starting to lead at younger ages and in different ways than I ever did at the same age. They have opportunities I never had, and they take chances I didn't. The people we love, young or old, need encouragement and nurturing. Be a friend in your family and in your close circles. We all have different talents to bless each other with so make sure to share yours as often as you can.

Some people are born with natural leadership qualities. They have charisma, confidence, and the ability to command a room. They are natural motivators and influencers. They have a knack for seeing the big picture and for making others see it too. But leadership is not just for the chosen few. It can be learned and developed. It can be honed through experience, through trial and error, through success and failure. No one will call you on your crap quicker than your family.

When I was young, I used to quote scripture, mostly proverbs, at my dad as excuses for why I wasn't getting along with my siblings. One of my favorites is Proverbs 17:17 (BRG), "A friend loveth at all times, and a brother is born for adversity." Sometimes families can feel like they are meant to make your life difficult. When done right, though? Families are the haven of our lives. They are there for the hardest times. In your family, you definitely learn what you are and are not capable of. I talk too much. I'm goofy. I'm weird — so my brothers say. I wish I could live all the time with the same giving energy my mom has. I see that I am sometimes too much like my dad in temperament. I always admired the cleverly creative brain and confidence of my brother. I was always jealous that my baby brother is one of the smartest people I know. My family is not surprised by the things I've done. They know me. There are definitely things about me that bug them, but we all respect and love each other. I believe leadership starts with those who are closest to you.

How do you treat those you say you love? Lead by example. What are your best qualities according to your family? If you don't have a family, you have a family of close friends. What do they say is your best quality? Do they support you in what you are trying to do? Lead where you stand. Authenticity cannot be faked around people who know you. The only way to prove yourself is by action. Live each day like the dream you know it can be. Leaders are tough. They make hard decisions and they prioritize. Show up for the people you need the most in your life.

NEXT STEPS

Find your personal strengths, learn to love in your family circle, and jump at opportunities that come your way within your community. Whether you are a born leader or a made one, remember that you can lead where you stand. You don't have to wait for a promotion or a title. You don't have to wait for someone to give you permission. You can start leading right now, right where you are.

You can lead by being a positive role model. You can lead by standing up for what you believe in. You can lead by helping others succeed. You can lead by making a difference in your own small way. So, don't underestimate your potential. Don't underestimate your ability to make a difference. Because no matter where you are, you can lead where you stand.

ABOUT ROBERT AYMAR

 It took much of Robert Aymar's lifetime and two handsome, falsely labeled grandsons to realize that there was no one in leadership today who would step up and speak the truth of our falsely labeled races. He believes that there is truth in the word of the Bible, which tells us that we are all made in the image of God. Being gifted with a sense of artistic vision that sees and interprets color in many avenues of life, he learned that his color sense was wrong in one key place: the four falsely labeled races of our world, Red, Black, White, and Yellow.

For more information regarding our authors, please visit our webpage! BestSellerPublishing.org/ExpertLeadership

CHAPTER 15

LEADING IN IMPORTANT CHANGES

(CLARIFYING THE PAST, SEEING THE PRESENT, AND COMMITTING TO THE FUTURE)

BY ROBERT AYMAR

Life has led me down a path where the labors of others paved a road for me to follow. I can only bear witness to all the things that led me to be here for others now, in a way I never thought I would.

I grew up in poorer neighborhoods where hustlers provided us citizens with many things for less than we could afford. There was never an open idea of being superior to others. However, there was this notion that people of other races did not mix.

As a child, I could draw well enough to understand there was something very wrong with me being "white," because a more accurate colored pencil was unavailable. I saw it as some strange, wrong placement from the start.

The TV was black and white, and the news of those days depicted the same ideals. At six years old, already I had to witness the civil discord created by a society filled with riots, abuse, and complaints about racism that spread like wildfire across America. On the screen, I saw the man, Rev. Dr. Martin Luther King Jr. leading those like him to protest without violence. I had only just learned prayer a few years before, which my father took no part in. He was an angry man, and Rev. King was non-violent. I began to have more honor for God and Rev. King than for my father.

The next event by Rev. King that I can remember molded me to see others in the way he spoke of in his speech about a dream he had. I must tell you and everyone who will hear me that it was neither a speech nor a dream; it was a prophecy that began the first day I and many others heard it.

As I said, my vision saw no black and white on people, so it was natural for me to believe Dr. King's words were for all. Judge only by character because the division of black and white was a lie. Did he say it was a lie then? No! But even at around seven years old, I believed it was.

As the years followed, I learned other things, like the concept of a "white lie." That harmless and trivial thing that many believe isn't so bad, but it is still a lie. That concept lingered in my mind until I finally wrote a book.

By the age of 15, I was hanging out in bars where, most of the time, no one was white — or at least they didn't fit the mold. I went to bars because I was a big boy then and, for whatever reason, I passed as old enough to be there. I drank beer and played pool with whoever was there to play against. There were never any problems, and we were always social, having a good time together.

After growing up in a world where side hustles were just how people experienced poverty, by the 1970s, the music and cultural environment of the world was changing fast, and so was I. From using marijuana to selling it was a natural step for me to take. I was young and poor, and if I wanted to smoke it, I had to sell it too. It was the natural order of the life I grew up in.

It became my way of life in a circle of friends who all enjoyed the same culture as I did almost daily. As the music changed, so did the drugs and the people. But one thing always stayed constant: I never lived in the world as if I were or had to be something separated by race.

In my book, I talk about these fences we have in society; well, I never had them and still don't. In the 1970s, many of us who were what we called "hippies" did not believe in the racial divide. So it was for most of us in the drug culture as well. There were good and bad people, just like good and bad dealers. However, none of us looked at it as black and white; we just dealt with one another. Plain and simply that!

I was arrested a couple of times and sent to prison twice into the 1980s. During those times of imprisonment, I never followed or became part of any racially separate group, as some do. There was the Aryan Brotherhood, which many prisoners, believing they were white, would join. However, I could not become part of that whole thing because I was born in Germany, and due to the historical context of World War II, my outlook differed significantly from their ideals.

Sure, I dealt with some racism while in jail, but that was the way they behaved due to their beliefs, not mine. By then, I had already begun to see that most of the racists were products of their upbringing or poor programming, as I would put it today. I, for one, was not a product of that; I may have been a product of my music and the culture of drug use, but I didn't divide humanity. I believed God made us all as one in His image, even then.

The year 1985 was monumental for me. I lived in the fast lane, and everything around me changed fast. Families in my life were mixing, and children were being born and called "biracial" as if it was the only way to distinguish them properly. These children were never that to me; they were my nieces and nephews or my friend's children who were part of my heart too.

I was dealing drugs now, interstate, near and far. Cocaine was the drug of choice, and I was even flying from New Jersey to Florida and back with drugs both ways. Back then, I was able to strap thousands of dollars in cash around my waist to carry concealed to buy drugs, and then I would do the same with the drugs to bring them back home again. I sometimes hid them in luggage, only to have some significant scares. I can tell you stories about those times. I lived on the edge every day.

I was married with one son, and the marriage was not going well. Was it the drugs and dealing, or was it, in truth, that the marriage was all wrong too? It certainly had to do with both things. And then, we were about to have another child together, on top of everything. I knew everything must change, but how and when weighed heavily on my mind.

I got this call from a friend in Virginia, and he said friends had been arrested, and he believed they had told on me too. As the tension grew,

I tried to make changes as if I had time. So many things had led up to this point, and there was a time I would have cleared inventory, but not that day.

So, it happened once again, busted for a third time. This time was different from all the rest. I faced a total of 145 years between two states, Virginia and New Jersey. There is so much I could share about all this, but now is not the time for any of that.

It is time to share a truth I have avoided over and over again. God has always been with me. Even when I would not follow Him, He would follow me. So, there He was, waiting for me to trust Him.

My brother-in-law Fred was God's voice, leading me home to become born again. Fred and I have been friends for a long time, and God led us both through a commitment I needed to make for my subsequent journeys.

I can assure you that God's Holy Spirit is real and came to me. I was at peace, and I faced life in prison till I would die and yet still felt calm. It's unbelievable in many ways but true.

I was under God's care, not my own or the courts. I faced a sentence under the RICO Act in New Jersey of a total of 35 years for a third-time conviction but only did 3 years. I served no time for my fourth conviction of kingpin charges in Virginia for the 110 years I would have faced.

Only by God's grace is a wretch like me saved. I genuinely confess I was guilty of all charges, so why? It was a question I lived with for another 30 years until now.

Fast-forwarding through three marriages to the present, my new marriage was conflicted on the topics of race and social status. My wife told me when we met that she had three degrees: one in teaching, another in psychology, and the last in employee law. The day I married her, she began using her third degree against me, all too often.

There were problems with my daughter, who has two children born out of wedlock who were falsely labeled — in my eyes — as biracial, but in my wife's eyes they were just that, biracial. So, my wife and I had our differences there too.

Next, my wife had problems during COVID-19 at work, where she reported racism against her by her newly hired superior. During that time, I heard many issues being raised during phone conversations, meetings, and side conversations. All I can say is I could sense both parties had their problems, which I could see as unorthodox behavior.

I began writing my memoirs to avoid all these outside pressures. I neither believed in her arguments nor did I wish to be a part of them. However, I kept getting writer's block and looking at a picture of my two youngest grandsons together. I began to wonder what the meaning behind it was.

Then, all around me, I could hear a voice telling me, *You know why? Because only you can do this.* Looking at my grandsons, the title of what I was to write came to me as if it fell from the sky or God: *The False Color Divide.*

Of course, I must give it to God because God, not man, created me to not believe in separate races. God also gave me the freedom to think I was right, even in a world where only those with excellent education lead societies, great and small.

So, I wrote a book for the first time in my life. God chose me to write to free the world from division, even in my divided house with my wife. I can tell you there was no ease in doing so, and my trials mounted each day till I left my new home and my new wife, never to see her again.

My lack of education has been an incredible blessing every day of my life. There is no hierarchy I fear because I always remember to forgive even educated people for believing the untrue. False news is not false news. It is news programmed to meet the approval of those who believes it serves them.

But I will always warn everyone: If you serve what is wrong, do you not serve what is unjust, too? The world has a more significant journey ahead than even I do because, long before me, many people feared being held liable for leading wrongly.

For those who fear judgment, remember always that God is behind us all, no matter what comes ahead. The future manages to be defined by the past: something behind us all in history, as told by men who were led unquestioningly by their own goals, not God's.

If a society's goal is to divide, then do not identify us as "we the people." Do not lie and talk about unity if that is not your only direction. America is imperfect, but its policies and politics should never divide its people by any lie ever again. We are, in fact, all one race indivisible by either the science of DNA or foolish word of mouth.

For those who wish to read my book, *The False Color Divide*, you do God and me a great honor in wanting to change the future to become the best it can one day — together for all. Many thanks to all who have given me your time and used your eyes to read about who I am and what I know to be true. We are all unique individuals who deserve to be free from racism.

For more information regarding our authors,
please visit our webpage!
BestSellerPublishing.org/ExpertLeadership

ABOUT DR. BENJAMIN KOEN

Dr. Ben Koen empowers elite performers — leaders, entrepreneurs, and professionals — to transform outer success into deep, lasting fulfillment across all six pillars of an extraordinary life — body, mind, spirit, emotions, relationships, and wealth. Through his proprietary SEA Method™ and groundbreaking Elite Life Code™ signature course that integrates discoveries from music, neuroscience, and holistic health, you eliminate the exact stressors holding you back today, optimize your well-being, and unlock your peak performance — delivering outcomes his clients describe as "the missing piece that made everything finally work."

For more information regarding our authors,
please visit our webpage!
BestSellerPublishing.org/ExpertLeadership

CHAPTER 16

UNLEASH LEADERSHIP WITHIN
(CUTTING-EDGE NEUROSCIENCE
AND THE SEA METHOD)

BY DR. BENJAMIN KOEN

In moments of distress, the human spirit often discovers its most profound truths. For me, as a young boy of just five years old, it was amidst the turmoil of my parents' arguments that I discovered a gateway to inner peace in a little bamboo grove behind our home in a small town in Georgia. That place became my oasis — a sacred space of healing and empowerment, and the catalyst for unleashing my leadership within.

Whenever any turmoil became overwhelming, a voice from within compelled me to steal away to my bamboo hideaway. Lying amidst the towering stalks, feeling the earth beneath me, I surrendered to that inner voice and to the music that nature was playing all around me — the rustle and dance of leaves in the breeze, the birds singing, and the gentle sway of the bamboo. With each breath, I felt peace returning to my body, relaxing every fiber of my being. As the stress melted away, my inner voice urged me to stay, to go deeper into that peaceful state. Gazing into the shimmering space above, beyond the tall bamboo, my mind and spirit expanded into the sky, absorbing the rays of the sun. Breathing deeper, slower, I felt a sense of renewal — joy, love, peace, and then ... freedom.

Later, back home, I realized that music provided the same transformative experience. I discovered that I could enter my bamboo sanctuary in my mind through music and sound, which helped me to hear my inner voice and find harmony. From this moment, I was consciously aware that I had a leader within — a guide I could always trust and rely on to lead me forward.

Music became my sacred space of meditation and transformation. Later in life, I realized that music had always been that for me from my earliest memories, long before I even knew the words *sacred, meditation,* or *transformation.* I knew that music was a vehicle that could transport me anywhere I wanted to go in my mind. Sometimes I would envision a kind of fantasy journey with no specific goal in mind, and other times, I would envision something specific that I longed for. I started to see a connection between what was happening in my music-meditation and the rest of life — the things I envisioned came true.

At times, my vision was realized immediately, and other times, it became manifest over longer periods of time. Little did I know at the time that these experiences would change me forever and set me on a lifelong journey exploring the inner world of the mind through music and meditation. This early experience laid the foundation for what would later become the See, Experience, Act (SEA) Method, a practice I created that is grounded in the power of music and meditation to foster leadership from within.

TAKING THE LEAD WITHIN

Years later, during my doctoral research and while refining my music-meditation practice, I discovered Hebb's law, a beautiful neurologic principle that sheds light on how music and meditation transform the brain, behavior, and life. It asserts that "neurons that fire together, wire together." This explains how repeated thoughts, feelings, and actions shape and create your reality.

This principle is evident in athletes, musicians, and experts who use practice and repetition to form neural patterns that lead to success. However, there's a misconception that practice makes perfect. If your practice is flawed, those mistakes become ingrained in your brain over time, reinforcing the very habits that hinder progress.

In your SEA Method meditation, regularly focusing on and feeling your desired outcome sends a message to your unconscious mind, prompting it to harness untapped potential to achieve your goals.

Simultaneously, you take conscious actions toward those goals. This dual approach aligns with Hebb's law, breaking old patterns and creating new pathways that foster your empowered leader within.

Through countless music-meditation sessions, I identified a pattern with three steps:

- See your vision clearly

- Experience and feel it fully in your body

- Act in alignment with it

These steps form the foundation of the SEA Method, which helps unlocks your inner leader to realize your personal and professional goals.

MUSIC-EMPOWERED LEADERSHIP

Before delving into the SEA Method, there are two crucial elements to consider for maximizing its impact.

First, when selecting music for your SEA Method meditation, you have four broad options: familiar music, unfamiliar music, the sounds of nature, and your own voice.

- **Familiar music:** This can be particularly powerful if it aligns closely with your personal or professional goals because it can reinforce the desired message in your unconscious mind.

- **Unfamiliar music:** Without prior associations, this can serve as an even more potent tool, helping to link your goal or vision to sound in a new and creative way. It taps into both your conscious and subconscious mind, allowing your creativity to flow.

- **Sounds of nature:** Nature sounds can also provide a profound meditative experience, creating a rich sensory landscape that fosters connection to your inner leader. Experiment with the limitless range of sounds and environments that resonate with you to enhance your meditation experience.

- **Your voice:** The vocal element here isn't about sing-ing, but about resonating with your own sound. Simply allow a sound to emerge from within and reverberate through your body and into the space around you. Start with a long, gentle hum or an open "Ah" sound. As you vocalize, take deep, relaxed breaths between each exhalation.

Second, choosing the right goal or vision is vital to your success. To help you clarify your focus, ask yourself one simple but powerful question:

As a leader, what is most important for me right now — to be, do, or have in my personal or professional life?

If you're uncertain, consider what matters most in the following six areas of life and how these aspects influence your leadership:

- BODY
- MIND
- SPIRIT
- EMOTIONS
- RELATIONSHIPS
- BUSINESS and WEALTH

Once you identify your goal or vision, visualize it with as much clarity and detail as possible. If it resonates deeply and feels aligned with your inner self, you're ready to begin practicing the SEA Method.

Integrate your chosen music into your SEA Meditation sessions both morning and evening, and commit to taking one to three action steps daily toward your goal. By aligning music, meditation, and action, you will not only unleash your leader within but also maximize your own potential and inspire the full potential in those you lead.

The Proven SEA Method:
See — Experience — Act

Prepare for Your SEA Meditation

If you know my Three-Breath Meditation, you can use that to prepare for your SEA Meditation or you can simply do the following:

- If you are going to use recorded music, turn it on now. If you use your voice, you can begin the gentle humming sound or open "Ah" sound now. Simply be in a comfortable position, take a few deep breaths, and with each breath relax more deeply.

- If you need to, you can do a few gentle stretches to increase your body awareness.

- Remember your most important goal or vision you chose above and bring it to the front of your mind and close your eyes.

Continue with the next three steps to do your SEA Meditation: See — Experience — Act.

SEA Meditation Method

1. See the end in the beginning

Close your eyes and see your goal or vision clearly in your mind now. Paint a picture or create a movie in your mind of what that looks and feels like. Let your emotions and feelings naturally grow as you move into the next step, Experience.

2. Experience and feel your vision as real, now in your body

Feel your vision of what you want to be, do, or have as a leader. Feel it in your body and experience your vision as though it is already fulfilled. Express and feel your gratitude for every step along the way and for being the leader you envisioned. Stay in this state for as long as you like while the music or your voice naturally carry the meaning and emotion of your vision deep into your unconscious mind and harmonize with your conscious mind. Fully enjoy this experience of what it feels like to have already achieved your goal and realized your vision. As you arise from your meditation, immediately take the third step, Action.

3. Act

Take daily action as though your goals and vision have already been achieved, and you are now the leader you envisioned. As you take consistent actions that are aligned with your vision, you will move in that direction until your vision is fully realized. Any limitations between your unconscious and conscious mind disappear, you attract the resources you need, and you become what you envision.

> *Do this SEA Meditation every morning and evening and remember it throughout your day.
> NOTE: Feel free to keep a SEA Meditation Journal of your experience of meditation and your experiences throughout the day.

Every morning, when you reach the Action stage of your SEA Meditation, extend the feeling from your meditation into every moment of your day. When you lose that feeling, which is natural and will happen, give your leader within a brain and body boost by doing this: simply recall your music in your mind (or listen to your music again) and reintegrate the high point of your meditation from the morning. Every night before you sleep, do your SEA Meditation and your unconscious mind will do its magic during your sleep state to build the neural networks that you are also developing during the morning meditation and aligned actions throughout the day.

I'M OKAY NOW ...

When I was 12, I was living in Ohio, and my parents had been divorced for four years. One summer evening, I was deeply saddened by the news that day that a friend of mine, Trent, was killed by a garbage truck while he was riding his bike near his home. As my feelings about his death mounted on my stress over my parents' problems, the sadness became too much. I needed more than my bamboo sanctuary, which I no longer had in my backyard. There was no special physical place to escape to, so I had to take a journey in my mind, and I instinctively turned to music. I remember the energy and feeling of that moment.

I closed the door to my bedroom, picked up my saxophone, and took a few deep breaths. Feeling the weight of the saxophone in my hands and inhaling its familiar and comforting fragrance increased the sense of anticipation for the healing journey I was about to experience. I knew it wouldn't be easy, but I welcomed it and instinctively knew I needed it.

I wet the cane reed in my mouth and put it on the saxophone mouthpiece. Without a song or plan in mind, I drew in a deep breath and began to play what I was feeling. I still remember the theme of the song of lament and love that flowed through me that evening and brought me healing, peace, and strength. But most important, I was connected and in conscious harmony with my inner voice — my leader within. I felt a sense of being in harmony with my whole being.

The emotions and energies from within me poured out — improvising and expressing my inner voice through music. Through improvisation, I was both playing my emotions and playing through them to the renewed state they were leading me to. After about an hour, I stopped playing and stayed in that meditative, generative space.

A knock at the door broke me out of that state, and my older brother entered. He had a look on his face that I had never seen before. "Ben, what was that? I loved it," he said.

"Just playing," I answered. There were a few tears on my face still, and I could feel a peaceful and vibrant energy inside me.

"That was beautiful ... are you okay?" he asked.

"Yeah, I am now."

Looking back on that experience, I saw that I could have an immediate realization or manifestation of my desired outcome if I was in harmony with my leader within. Later, I would learn through studying music, the brain, and behavior that one way of understanding this conversation with an inner voice is the interaction between the conscious and unconscious aspects or dimensions of the mind. Think of the conscious mind as the steering wheel and the unconscious mind as the engine.

Both need to work together in harmony to move you toward your destination. As I explored this area more deeply, I realized that in the space where the conversation between conscious and unconscious happens, there is a leader that emerges when harmony is reached between the conscious and unconscious mind, and that music-meditation is a powerful vehicle for creating this harmony.

But more importantly for you, in your journey to find or strengthen your leader within, I discovered that when you can see and connect the meaning and feeling of your vision to your music-meditation experience, your leader within becomes fully present, and you maximize your potential. This enables you to take action and realize your goals and vision with newfound gratitude, wisdom, and awareness.

When you deeply integrate your envisioned leader into your morning meditation, extend your leader into your daily actions, and revisit and strengthen your leader in your nighttime meditation, which naturally extends into your sleep state where your unconscious mind draws freely on your untapped leadership potential, you create a cycle of consistent and limitless growth as a leader.

AFTERWORD

BY BOB HARPOLE, OPERATIONS
MANAGER, BEST SELLER PUBLISHING

I've had the unique privilege of overseeing the development of many powerful books in my time with Rob and Best Seller Publishing. I have watched authors struggle to find content. I've walked with them through impostor syndrome and writer's block. It's always a joy to see the book come to life eventually. I must say that this particular book has left a lasting impression on me, both professionally and personally.

There is an amazing diversity of voices in this book. But what really struck me was how sincere and authentic the stories were. There wasn't a lot of corporate jargon or generic advice. Honesty and vulnerability shine through. I admire that so many authors share their struggles. Beyond that, they share the ways that they have struggled, adapted, and grown. I appreciate that each contributor was generous enough to share those crucial lessons with us.

I thrive as a "behind-the-scenes" person. My greatest joy is seeing others succeed. So, it was an unexpected pleasure to have this book have such a big impact on me. It inspires me to be a more effective leader in my role within the company.

A few themes really stuck with me:

> **Leadership is personal.** I was inspired by R.J. De Rossi's story of struggling to find his footing in a high-pressure role. I was moved by Jennifer Knowles's story of turning a moment of injustice into a national movement. This book makes a compelling argument that leadership doesn't stem from a title. It comes from our response when things become difficult.

Context matters. Neil Gordon's chapter on the importance of context helped me see that even the best intentions can fall flat if we don't frame them properly. It's not just about what you say—it's about how, when, and why you say it.

Mastery takes humility. It was striking that nearly every author emphasized the importance of learning. I read stories of learning through failure, feedback, or confronting something entirely new. That is wonderfully refreshing and encouraging.

I'm reminded by this book that leadership isn't just for CEOs of Fortune 500 companies. You don't have to be a household name to influence others. No, leadership is something each of us can practice every day. Maybe you're managing a team. Maybe you're raising a family. Maybe you are one of those CEOs who have thousands of lives under your direction. Regardless, this book will help us seize the unique opportunities to lead with our minds, mastery, and meaning.

I hope you'll take away as much from these pages as I did. And maybe, like me, you'll be inspired to lead differently tomorrow than you did today.

Bob Harpole

For more information regarding our authors,
please visit our webpage!
BestSellerPublishing.org/ExpertLeadership